D0281579

THE
GUIDE
BADGE
BOOK

published by The Guide Association,
17-19 Buckingham Palace Road,
London SW1W 0PT

ISBN 0 85260 113 1

Illustrated by Sue Faulks
Designed by Caroline Marklew
Edited by Gillian Sutton

© The Guide Association, 1995
Reprinted with corrections 1995

Guiders are reminded that during the life span of this publication policy changes may be made by The Guide Association which will affect the accuracy of information within these pages.

Printed and bound in Scotland by Scotprint Ltd

INTRODUCTION

- Do you have a particular interest or hobby? Can you find a badge syllabus in this book which covers that interest?

- Is there something you have always wanted to try? Is there a badge that you could do to help you learn about that topic?

- Have you already done something that could be counted towards gaining a badge?

In this book you will find details of all the Interest Badges, Service Badges, Collective Emblems, Patrol Interest Pennants and other badges you may gain as a Guide. You may choose to take as many or as few as you like and they represent one particular part of the wide programme available to you as a Guide. Once you have satisfactorily met the requirements for the badge you will be awarded a cloth badge to wear on your sash.

When you choose to work on an Interest Badge it may be because you already know a lot about the particular subject or because it is a new area that you wish to explore. In both cases you will be required to work hard, either to improve the standard you have achieved or to reach an acceptable standard. The tester will be judging your individual effort rather than assessing you against a set standard.

If you choose to take a Service Badge you will need to reach the high standard set for all the challenges in the badge. This is because, when you wear the badge on your sash, you and other people need to be confident that you could put your knowledge and skills into practice if you were involved in a real life emergency. In addition you will need to be re-tested every two years to ensure that your knowledge is up-to-date.

For some of the badges you are asked to write things down. You may do this in any way you choose, for example using a computer, word processor or special typewriter rather than handwriting. You may also communicate by using a sign language or Braille, art or collage work. If you are not physically able to do a required clause in a badge you can instruct another person instead or your Guider and the tester may adapt that particular clause to meet your needs or set another equally challenging clause.

You will normally be tested by someone, other than your Guider, who is an expert in the particular subject. The test will be an opportunity for you to talk with this person about your hobby or interest.

You will see from the illustrations that some of the badges are staged badges. This is because they have three or four stages and you can get a badge for each stage. You do not have to start at Stage 1 and you do not have to work through each stage unless you want to. You start at the stage that is right for you – for instance you might already be an experienced Church Bellringer so could start Stage 2 of the Bellringer Badge. On the other hand you might have just learned how to knit so would start at Stage 1 of the Knitter syllabus. If you have already achieved a staged badge whilst in Brownies you might want to take a more advanced stage as a Guide.

Patrol Interest Pennants and the Patrol Purpose Patch are gained by working with the rest of your Patrol on particular areas that interest you all. When you have completed them, each person who took part may wear the appropriate badge on her sash.

In this book you will find that some of the badges have notes or hints which will help you find the information you need to pass the badge. Where there are no notes you should talk to your Guider, your teacher or instructor or go to the local library for information. You may also be able to find some of the books referred to in your local library. Ask your Guider if she has Guide Association publications which you can borrow or send for a free catalogue to: The Guide Association Trading Service, Atlantic Street, Broadheath, Altrincham, Cheshire WA14 5EQ. Guide Association publications are available from Trading Service, Guide shops and depots.

Badges will be tested in your first language. You do not have to take the tests in English if this is not your native language, although you may choose to take them in English. Remember it is your choice.

Start off by looking through this book and seeing how many varied and interesting subjects are covered and think how much you could gain by working on some of these areas. You will find that all of the Eight Points: enjoying the out of doors, keeping fit, thinking for yourself, giving service, exploring the arts, becoming a homemaker, keeping the Guide Law and getting to know people are covered. There is also plenty of variety whether you are a beginner or an expert in the subject you have chosen.

So now it's over to you!

CONTENTS

6

ACCIDENT PREVENTION

Choose three clauses from the following:

Present your findings in an interesting way.

1 Know what special precautions to take in a house with:

a small children

b old people

c people with a disability.

Design a 'Home Safety Check'.

2 Know and where possible demonstrate how to prevent accidents:

a in a family living room

b in a garden (including shed and greenhouse)

c at a hazardous local feature, for example a canal, building site or farm.

3 Know three different ways of preventing accidents when involved with each of the following :

a fireworks

b boating and bathing

c public transport, cars and cycles

d animals.

4 Using press cuttings and case studies, produce a profile of road accidents involving your own age group. Use categories such as: male/female, location, time, circumstances and vehicles. How would you encourage your friends to be more aware of these facts?

5 Choose a section of a street or road that you know well. Identify possible dangers that might affect:

a elderly people

b children

c disabled people.

6 With a group of friends, prepare a short discussion (similar to radio interviews) discussing personal experiences of childhood accidents in the home. Play it to your Unit.

7 Prepare a talk, using photographs, slides, video etc, showing simple precautions for parents collecting young children from school.

Date:...............................

....
Tester's signature

....
My signature

AGILITY

1 Bring a certificate to the test to show that you have done one of the following in the last 12 months:

a walk 6 metres over a rope bridge

b climb 3 metres up a rope

c swim 25 metres

d cover 2km at Scout's pace (walk 20 paces, run 20 paces).

2 Pass eight of the following clauses at the test. Show good control and posture in everything you do.

a Demonstrate good walking and running.

b Turn a rope backwards and skip continuously for one minute.

c Demonstrate slow and fast movements in a wheelchair.

d In a wheelchair show skill in following an obstacle course which should include ramps

a

7

up and down and forward and backward gates.

e Throw a lifeline within easy reach of a person 7 metres away.

f Throw a hard ball overarm to land between two side-lines 3.5 metres apart.

g Catch a hard ball from quick short throws and from high throws.

h With a tennis ball and from a distance of 6 metres, hit a target 30cm square.

i Perform a balancing feat on the floor.

j Do a handstand.

k Leapfrog in good style.

l With your feet together, jump over an obstacle 30cm high ten times.

m Balance a wheelchair on its back wheels for 30 seconds.

n Climb in and out of a wheelchair from floor level.

o Go up and down a 7.62cm-12.7cm kerb in a wheelchair.

p Run whilst bouncing a ball (as in basketball).

q Perform a jogging sequence lasting one minute. You should move forwards and sideways and show agility in linking movements.

Date: 1/3/95

Tester's signature

K Thomson

My signature

Liane Ireland

AIRCRAFT

1 Know and be able to identify the different characteristics of five types of aircraft, e.g. helicopter, light aircraft, freighter, commercial transport aircraft, military aircraft, glider, training aircraft.

2 Identify the following parts on an aircraft: fuselage, wing leading edge, wing trailing edge, aileron, rudder, fin, tail plane, elevator, flap, engine nacelle and undercarriage.

3 Explain what is meant by the following terms: banking, looping, yawing, rolling, side-slipping, stalling, spinning.

4 Understand the effect of wind on a light aeroplane when it is taking off and landing. Improvise a wind indicator.

5 Talk to your Patrol about the history of flying and make a model or drawing of an incident in the history of flying.

Date:..............................

....
Tester's signature

....
My signature

ANGLER

1 Fish for one season and keep brief records. If possible, belong to your local angling club.

2 Have a working knowledge of licence laws and fishing rights. Know the Country Code and be aware of conservation issues which relate to angling.

3 Be able to keep afloat and swim 25 metres breast stroke.

4 Have a knowledge of fish in your district and:

a Know which baits are suitable for catching each fish and where these baits are usually found (include ground-baiting methods).

b Know the types of tackle suitable for each species and be able to tackle up for them.

c Explain the methods most suitable for catching each species of fish.

5 Know which knots are most suitable for tying nylon lines etc, and be able to do running repairs to tackle and rods.

6 Understand the precautions to be taken in, on or beside water and the potential hazards associated with the use of specialist equipment.

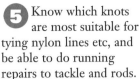

Date:..............................

....
Tester's signature

....
My signature

AQUARIST

Note: *You can take this badge with either cold water or tropical fish.*

1 Own or part-own, an aquarium of not less than 27 litres, i.e. 45cm x 25cm x 25cm. Be responsible for its total care and maintenance for at least six months. The tester will inspect your aquarium at the beginning and end of the six-month period.

2 Understand the general requirements for setting up an aquarium and maintaining it. Identify six plants, three rooted and three cuttings.

3 Explain and demonstrate the use of a thermometer, siphon, planting stick, magnetic cleaner.

4 Know the cause and treatment for a number of common diseases including white spot, fungus and dropsy.

5 Recognise four varieties of cold water fish and eight tropical fish and name the area of the world they originate from. Know how regularly and what amount fish should be fed.

6 Explain the advantages and disadvantages of using:

a a mechanical filter

b a biological filter.

7 At the test identify two types of live food and two species of plants and demonstrate the use of a siphon.

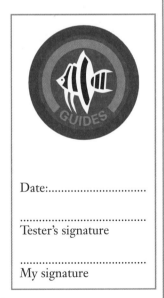

Date:..............................

....
Tester's signature

....
My signature

ARTIST

1 Bring examples of your work to the test. They should be at least 22cm x 18cm in size, in three different media and showing three different subjects such as landscape, portrait, figures, still life, abstract. At least one of your pieces must show the use of colour.

2 Bring to the test one of the following:

[a] a detailed drawing, in pencil, pen, ink or charcoal, of different parts of plants or flowers

b experiments in textural patterns. You could use rubbings, string prints, waste-card prints, glass prints etc.

c a decorative panel, at least 22cm x 18cm in size, using materials such as coloured papers, kitchen foil, rope, string, fabric, bark, feathers, wool.

3 At the test observe and illustrate a figure, still life or landscape in front of you. The tester will choose the subject after she/he has seen the work you submitted for Clauses 1 and 2. You will have to choose and provide your own medium (perhaps water colours, tempera, poster paint, crayons, pastels, chalk, ink, collage or charcoal) and produce a piece of artwork at least 22cm x 18cm in size.

4 Tell the tester of one occasion during the last 12 months when you used your artistic talent to contribute to your Patrol or Company programme.

Date: 12/5/95

....
Tester's signature
....
My signature

BAND

To qualify for this badge, you must complete one of the Parts.

Part I Marching Bands

1 Play regularly in a marching band.

2 Play three prepared pieces for a total duration of six to nine minutes. The pieces must display a fair amount of pitch, dynamics, rhythmic content and good tonal control.

3 Explain the rudiments of musical notation necessary for you to play a piece from notation (not sight reading). This should cover:

a the lines and spaces of a stave including the clefs

b note values

c time and key signatures.

4 Explain the range of notes of your instrument in relation to a piano (organ) keyboard. If you are a drummer, you must know about flams, drags and paradiddles. You must also be able to play a good smooth roll with crescendo and diminuendo.

Part II Drum Major

1 Play regularly in a marching band.

2 Name up to six instruments which are played in the band.

3 Lead and direct the band on parade displaying the following:

a drill and deportment

b mace drill – correct signs for halt, mark time, cut off music etc.

c words of command:

- band – by the centre (left or right), quick march
- band – left (or right) wheel
- band – halt.

Part III Band

1 Play regularly in a band.

2 Play three prepared pieces for a total duration of six to nine minutes. The pieces must display a fair amount of pitch, dynamics, rhythmic content and good tonal control.

3 Explain the rudiments of musical notation necessary for you to play a piece from notation (not sight reading). This should cover:

a the lines and spaces of a stave including the clefs

b note values

c time and key signatures.

4 Explain the range of notes of your instrument in relation to a piano (organ) keyboard. If you are a drummer, you must know about flams, drags and paradiddles. You must also be able to play a good smooth roll with crescendo and diminuendo.

Date:..............................

....

Tester's signature

....

My signature

BELLRINGER
Church Bellringing

Notes

- *For all stages you should show that you attend practices and Service ringing regularly.*

- *It may be necessary to do some of the clauses at a tower other than your own.*

Stage 1

1 Ring rounds correctly, leading and following.

2 Lower a bell unaided.

3 Be able to follow simple call changes accurately and explain the difference between two named change patterns such as 'Queens', 'Tittums', 'Whittingtons' and 'Reverse Queens'.

4 Name the parts of a tower bell and explain the function of each. Explain how the revolution of the bell produces hand and back strokes.

5 Explain how bells are made and tuned.

6 Know where the six nearest peals of bells to your home tower are, the number of bells in each and the weight of the Tenor.

If possible, visit and ring rounds at two of these and tell the tester of your experiences.

Stage 2

1 Raise a bell unaided.

2 Show that you can put a 'whipping' on a rope end.

3 Know the importance of rope maintenance and how to change a rope.

4 Read a book on the history of bells or bellringing.

5 Be able to tell the tester about your local ringing association, e.g. its name, membership requirements, the name of the Ringing Master and the Secretary.

6 Visit and ring at six towers other than your own.

7 *Either*

For a Call Change Tower, ring an inside bell for the

b calling of a minimum of 60 changes.

or

For a Change Ringing Tower, ring an inside bell for the calling of a minimum of 60 changes.

or

For a Change Ringing Tower ring the treble to a touch of Plain Minor and an 'inside' bell to a plain course of a Doubles method.

Show that you know what is meant by 'passing the treble' and explain how this is used to assist in the ringing of two methods.

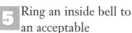**Stage 3**

1 Ring up and down in peal.

2 Show that you can complete long and short splices.

3 Know about the history of the bells in your own tower, and write an article about it for your church magazine or newsletter.

Either

For a Call Change Tower:

4 Conduct a touch.

5 Ring an inside bell to an acceptable competition standard. The bells should start and finish in the down position and a minimum of 60 changes should be used.

or

For a Change Ringing Tower:

6 Conduct 120 changes of Doubles from a bell affected at calls.

7 Ring a quarter peal.

8 Ring 720 changes of a Minor method inside.

Stage 4

1 Demonstrate the ability to complete an eye splice.

2 Spend a total of three hours in direct contact with visitors or ringing learners at open events or ringing training sessions.

3 Write an article (such as might be published in your church magazine) for possible ringing recruits, explaining how they will be taught.

Either

For a Call Change Tower:

4 Conduct 'Sixty on Thirds' from memory.

5 Lead up *and* down in peal.

or

For a Change Ringing Tower:

6 Conduct 720 changes of Minor.

7 Lead up *or* down in peal.

8 Ring the plain course of a Surprise method on an inside bell and be able to write out one lead of a Surprise method which you have not rung, starting only with the place notation. Draw the line for a working bell and mark the place bells.

Change Ringing on Handbells

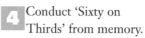**Stage 1**

1 Name five parts of a handbell, and describe how it is rung for change ringing.

2 Describe the system of numbering used in the set of bells which you ring.

3 Explain the technical terms used in ringing in your group.

4 Show that you understand the importance of care and maintenance of the metal and moving parts of a handbell.

5 With rhythmical precision, ring a pair of handbells correctly in rounds.

6 Show that you have attended a group on a regular basis.

Stage 2

1 Name six parts of a handbell and describe

how it is rung for change ringing.

2 Describe two systems of numbering used in handbell ringing.

3 Show that you know the importance of handbell care, maintenance and adjustment.

4 With rhythmical precision – using the hand stroke and back stroke positions – ring a pair of handbells correctly in rounds.

5 Show that you have attended a group on a regular basis.

Stage 3

1 Be able to give a short talk on the history of the handbell to a Ranger Unit or similar group.

2 Explain the technical terms used in ringing in your group.

3 Ring a pair of handbells using two methods, including 'Bobs' and 'Singles', consisting of 120 changes on five bells

and 720 changes on six bells.

4 Show that you have attended a group on a regular basis.

Tune Ringing on Handbells or Chimes

Stage 1

1 Name three parts of a handbell or chime and describe/demonstrate the method of ringing that your team usually uses for tune ringing.

2 Show that you understand the importance of the care and maintenance of the metal and moving parts of a handbell or chime.

3 Be able to read and explain simple music written in one of the following:

a staff notation

b tonic sol-fa notation

c alphabetical notation

d numerical notation.

4 Handling at least two handbells or chimes and reading from one of the notations listed above, play three tunes.

5 Show that you have attended a group on a regular basis for at least two months.

Stage 2

1 Be able to complete all requirements listed for Stage 1.

2 *Either*

Name six parts of a

handbell and explain their functions.

or

Name the main parts of a handchime and explain their functions.

3 Handling at least two handbells or chimes and reading from one of the notations given in Stage 1 Clause 3, play a selection of four tunes to include:

a a tune involving half beats

b a tune involving a repeat, where you play a section again

c two tunes in simple harmony.

4 Take part in a public performance, playing at least three tunes.

5 Take part in the regular cleaning/maintenance routines used by your team.

6 Show that you have attended a group on a regular basis for at least three months.

b

Stage 3

1 Be able to complete all requirements listed for Stage 2.

2 Show that you know how to keep handbells or chimes in good working order, including simple 'first aid' measures of repair that can be safely used, storage, etc.

3 Handling at least two handbells or chimes and using one of the notations listed in Stage 1 Clause 3, ring a programme of tunes lasting at least ten minutes. The programme should demonstrate full use of changes in tempo (speed), dynamics (loud and soft playing) and ringing techniques, e.g. shakes, damping, etc.

4 *Either*

Arrange a tune in simple harmony and teach it to your group.

or

Give a short talk on the history and development of handbells or chimes to a Ranger Unit or similar group.

5 Show that you have attended a group on a regular basis for at least six months.

Date:..............................

....
Tester's signature Stage 1

....
Tester's signature Stage 2

....
Tester's signature Stage 3

....
Tester's signature Stage 4

....
My signature

BIRD WATCHER

Hint Information can be obtained from The Royal Society for the Protection of Birds, The Lodge, Sandy, Bedfordshire, SG19 2DL.

Stage 1

1 Keep a list of birds which can be seen around your home during one month.

2 Keep a notebook on at least three bird-watching expeditions and show this to the tester. The notebook should contain date, time, place, weather, which species of bird you saw, and what they were doing.

3 Talk to the tester about ways of watching birds without disturbing them.

4 Tell the tester how you can help birds in both summer and winter.

5 Find out if there is a club for young ornithologists in your area.

Stage 2

1 Show the tester the equipment you use for bird watching. Include clothing, and reference books and binoculars if you have them. Show that you can use binoculars correctly.

2 Keep a notebook on at least ten bird-watching outings. Identify the birds you see and observe and describe some bird behaviour. Talk about your observations with the tester.

3 Make a simple chart showing the birds which you see around your home. Mark on the chart the months when you see them.

4 Draw a rough outline of a bird and mark on it the following parts: crown, back, rump, belly, breast, primaries, flank.

5 Be prepared to identify the pictures of ten species of birds common to your area.

14

6 Tell the tester about some local places where you go to watch birds, which species visit these places and which nest there.

Stage 3

1 Demonstrate the use and care of your bird-watching equipment. Tell the tester about the bird books you use and how and when you use them. Explain what is meant by the 'scientific order' which is used in most books.

2 Keep notes for at least six months on birds (and other wildlife) you see and interesting behaviour you observe. Use illustrations as well as written notes. Show the notebook to the tester and discuss entries.

3 Carry out a simple survey of birds visiting a particular study area: your parish, a local park or some other place you visit regularly (a larger area than a garden is necessary). Your survey could be a series of counts, a census of birds

during the breeding season, a line transect or some other generally accepted form of survey.

4 Draw the rough outline of a bird and mark on it the following parts: crown, rump, beak, belly, breast, primaries, flank, upper tail, coverts, tarsus speculum, supercilium, eye-stripe, nape, mantle, secondaries and wing coverts.

5 Demonstrate to the tester that you understand what is meant by migration. Explain the methods by which ornithologists have found out about birds' migration journeys. Name five summer migrants and five winter migrants which you could reasonably expect to see in your local area.

6 Describe some British habitats and explain the threats to them. Which species of bird are endangered by these changes?

7 Describe how a nature reserve can be managed (looked after and developed) to make it more suitable for birds. Tell the tester about any reserves that you have visited and your impressions of them.

Stage 4

1 Show the tester your bird-watching equipment, clothing and the books you find most useful. Discuss why and when you use particular books. Explain the order in which species are generally placed.

Also, discuss the merits (or otherwise) of optical equipment. Explain the magnification of binoculars and the occasions when a telescope can be useful.

2 Show the tester your notebook(s) covering a full year's bird watching.

Illustrations and written notes about numbers and behaviour should all be included. Discuss the excursions with the tester.

3 Be prepared to identify by sight, 20 or more species, most of which are found in the United Kingdom, but also a few others which are only rare visitors or species found mainly in mainland Europe. Say which are resident, summer migrants, passage migrants, etc. Also be prepared to identify or to be asked to describe the songs and calls of not more than ten common species.

4 Carry out voluntary work on a bird reserve or nature reserve. Discuss with your tester the importance of the reserve for wildlife and give an account of your activities.

5 Choose five species of bird which are threatened in the United Kingdom. Discuss the threats and the possible solutions with the tester.

6 Discuss with the tester the various types of

census and surveys that amateurs can help with.

7 Use your knowledge of, and interest in, ornithology to help another person prepare for Stage 1 or Stage 2 of this badge.

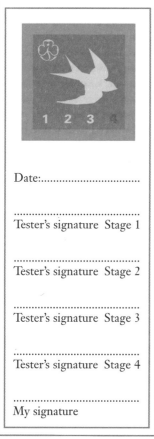

Date:..............................

....
Tester's signature Stage 1

....
Tester's signature Stage 2

....
Tester's signature Stage 3

....
Tester's signature Stage 4

....
My signature

CAMPER

1 Spend at least two consecutive nights under canvas in a Guide camp. Take part in camp activities and duties.

2 Help pitch and strike a tent.

3 Set and light a fire (either a camp fire or one for cooking).

4 Help your Patrol cook, serve and clear away a meal.

5 Tie up your bedding roll correctly and know how to look after your personal gear.

6 Make a simple gadget to use in a camp.

7 Know simple first aid for treating cuts, stings, bruises and burns.

Date: 1/2/96

....
Tester's signature

E. Todd
....
My signature
Liane Ireland

CAMPER ADVANCED

Note *The tester must hold the Camper's Licence or be an experienced camper.*

1 Bring to the test a certificate from your Guider or a qualified camper with whom you have camped, stating that you have proved yourself to be useful and reliable and recommending you as a candidate for the badge.

2 Go to two or more Guide camps. Altogether you must have spent at least six nights in a Guide camp.

3 Take part in:

a pitching, airing and striking a tent

b erecting, striking and packing up the screening or cubicles and poles in your own unit. You must know the skills required to do this.

4 Know how to care for tents, ground sheets, bedding and latrines in all types of weather. Show how to carry out emergency repairs to a tent, for example replace a guy line, improvise a tent peg, stick a small patch.

5 Make a gadget or gadgets using at least two of the following lashings: square, tripod and snake.

6 Construct a fireplace for cooking. Collect and stack suitable wood and light a wood fire out of doors. Know what safety precautions to take when you are lighting fires. Also know how to use a portable cooking stove and the safety precautions necessary when using it.

On your own fire and/or stove:

a Cook a meal for at least two people using a variety of cooking methods, for example frying, stewing or boiling.

b Know the safety precautions to take when cooking out of doors.

7 Understand how to store food, including bread, butter, milk and meat and how to dispose of all kinds of refuse.

Date:.............................

....
Tester's signature

....
My signature

CANOEIST

Where there is reason to believe that the level of water pollution or low temperatures may render capsize drill potentially hazardous, alternative safer locations including swimming pools may be used for those clauses marked with an asterisk.

Note *The abbreviation BCU has been used for the British Canoe Union throughout this syllabus.*

Stage 1

Notes

- *If you hold the BCU 1 Star or BCU Grade 1 Placid Water Test and complete Clause 1, you may have this badge.*

- *The test may be taken in a canoe or kayak with an open or closed cockpit on still water. A spray-deck need not be worn.*

- *The tester for Clauses 2 to 8 should hold BCU Supervisor (Leader), Placid Water Teacher, Instructor or higher qualification, or be a person with experience or a qualification approved by the County Assistant Outdoor Activities Adviser (Boating). The tester should look for performance at the standard expected for BCU 1 Star or Placid Water Tests Grade 1.*

1 Swim 50 metres and stay afloat for five minutes wearing clothes. This clause may be done in a swimming pool and you may wear a buoyancy aid if you wish.

2 Wear suitable clothing and a buoyancy aid for the test and be able to explain their importance to the tester. Know how to check your boat is safe before going afloat.

3 Launch the canoe and get into it.

4 Demonstrate alone or with a partner of similar ability:

a forward paddling over at least 100 metres

b paddling backwards

c paddling a circuit or figure-of-eight course using controlled turns

d stopping

e turning 360° using sweep strokes.

5 Show that you have made a satisfactory beginning in draw stroke, stern rudder and a support stroke.

6 Return to the edge and get out.

7 Know what to do if you capsize. If using a closed-cockpit kayak, demonstrate how to capsize and swim ashore. *

8 Know the Canoeist's Code of Conduct.

9 Hold a small first aid kit and know how to use it correctly.

Stage 2

Notes

• *If you hold the BCU 2 Star or the BCU Grade 2 or 3 Placid Water Test or BCU Grade 2 Surf Test and pass Clauses 1 and 9 above, you may have this badge.*

• *The tester for Clauses 2 to 9 should be qualified as BCU Instructor, Placid Water Instructor or higher BCU qualification, or a person holding a qualification, approved by the County Assistant Outdoor Activities Adviser (Boating). This person may also test Clause 1. The tester should look for performance at the standard expected for BCU 2 Star or Grade 2 or 3 Placid Water Tests.*

1 Swim 50 metres and stay afloat for five minutes wearing clothes. This clause may be done in a swimming pool and you may wear a buoyancy aid if you wish.

2 Show the tester your clothing and equipment and discuss why it is safe and suitable. Show some knowledge of the clothing and buoyancy aids for different conditions and of the materials used for boats and paddles.

3 Launch and get into your canoe. Fit a spray-deck if appropriate.

4 Demonstrate alone or with a partner of similar ability:

a efficient forward paddling over at least 200 metres.

b paddling backwards (keeping the boat straight while showing good paddling style)

c paddle a figure-of-eight course demonstrating relevant skills. Doubles partners must paddle both back and front.

d draw strokes on both sides keeping the boat in a straight line

e support strokes on both sides stationary and on the move (in a kayak show high and low brace)

f stern rudder

g 'J' stroke, if tested in an open canoe.

5 Show a satisfactory beginning in *two* of the following:

a sculling draw and sculling for support in a kayak

b sculling and cross-deck sculling in an open canoe

c eskimo rescue*

d ferry glide

e breaking into and out of moving water

f bow cut (bow rudder).

6 Go ashore showing correct approach relative to wind and current and get out.

7 Know what to do if you capsize and

• if using a kayak demonstrate capsize with spray-deck fitted, being rescued and getting back into your boat in deep water, and rescuing another paddler in deep water*

• if using an open canoe, jump out and climb back in unaided.*

8 Know the Canoeist's Code of Conduct. Answer questions about safety and access in the area where you paddle (e.g. dangers of weirs, currents, tides, group control and signs, the effect of weather, launching sites, access agreements).

9 Know how to recognise and deal with hypothermia. Describe to the tester the injuries that might happen when canoeing and what you would do.

Stage 3

Notes

• *If you hold the BCU 3 Star, Inland Proficiency, Sea Proficiency or both Grades 2 and 3 of Placid Water Tests and complete Clause 1 below, you may have this badge.*

• *The tester for Clauses 2 to 8 should hold a qualification as BCU Senior Instructor or one approved by the County Assistant Outdoor Activities Adviser (Boating).*

1 Swim 50 metres and stay afloat for five minutes wearing clothes. This clause may be done in a swimming pool and you may wear a buoyancy aid if you wish.

2 Present yourself for the test suitably dressed and equipped and you should be able to explain your choice of gear to the tester.

3 Launch your boat and get in. Return to shore and get out.

4 Paddling alone, demonstrate that you are proficient at moving and controlling the canoe using all the following strokes appropriate to your boat – forward paddling, reverse paddling, sweep strokes, draw strokes, stern rudder, recovery strokes, sculling draw, sculling for support, bow rudder/bow cut, cross-bow cut, bow draw (open canoe), emergency stop, backwater stroke/cross-deck backwater stroke, 'J' stroke.

5 Capsize, swim ashore and empty your canoe with assistance if required. *

6 Capsize in deep water and be rescued by another paddler. *

7 Rescue another paddler from deep water. (Another person may

be asked to help you but you must remain in charge of the rescue.) *

8 Answer questions to show that you know about:

a   the Canoeist's Code of Conduct

b   types of canoe and paddle

c   the river grading system and access to local waters

d   how to paddle in a group

e   use of tow lines

f   the hazards that may be encountered on open water, rivers and sea

g   specific local features

h   the general effect of tide, wind and current

i   where to obtain weather forecasts and information.

9 Know how to recognise and deal with hypothermia.

Demonstrate what you would do:

a   to stop bleeding

b   to identify and treat a broken bone

c   to treat an unconscious breathing patient.

Using a manikin show how to give expired air resuscitation.

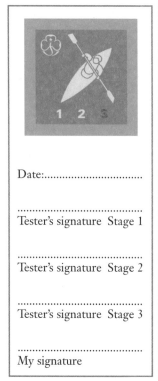

Date:................................

....
Tester's signature Stage 1

....
Tester's signature Stage 2

....
Tester's signature Stage 3

....
My signature

19

CARE OF ELDERLY PEOPLE

1 Find out what facilities and organisations are available in your District for elderly people, e.g. residential homes, clubs, day centres, Help the Aged, WRVS meals on wheels and so on. Learn more about one of them.

2 Tell the tester about one of the following:

a the causes and signs of hypothermia in an older person

b how to summon help for an old person who has fallen or is unwell

c what self aids are available for the elderly, e.g. long reachers, bath aids.

3 With the help of your Guider, arrange to meet the person in charge of a day centre, residential home or club for elderly people. Discuss with her/him any help you can give to those present, such as serving tea, arranging flowers, talking to residents about the past or other topics, taking an activity or game with a group, doing some task for them. Do this four times, perhaps taking members of your Patrol along too.

4 At your test, tell the tester how you have helped elderly people during your visits and anything you have learned from them.

Date:.............................

....
Tester's signature

....
My signature

CARPENTER

You may use electrical appliances if you have had adequate training or are supervised by an adult.

Ensure all safety precautions are taken when doing this badge.

Demonstrate your skill as a carpenter by doing four of the following:

1 Put together a 'flat pack' item of furniture.

2 Make and fix a shelf with ends.

3 Make a wooden box to show use of screws, nails, sanding, sawing and a method of making corners.

4 Fix a new piece of wood into an existing structure e.g. chair leg, window frame.

5 Carve, using knife and/or chisel, an object or animal.

6 Explain the following terms: sustainable forestry, knots and veneers.

7 Using pictures, photographs or samples explain the difference between pine, oak, beech and mahogany timbers and their uses.

8 Use a jig saw to cut animal shapes to use as templates for a Noah's Ark. Don't forget to sand the edges.

9 Design and construct a bar stool or equivalent.

10 Make an article of your own choice.

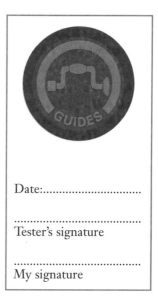

Date:.............................

....
Tester's signature

....
My signature

CHALLENGE

Notes

- *Choose and pass eight clauses. One clause must be chosen from each part.*

- *Part of this badge may be tested by your Unit Guider, provided at least two clauses are tested by an outside tester.*

Part I

1. Cover 1.6km (1 mile) in 12 minutes using Scout's pace (run 20 paces, walk 20 paces). Remember and deliver a verbal message.

2. Learn to swim 25 metres, or if you can already swim, learn life-saving backstroke or sidestroke and tow someone of your own size using a buoyant aid.

3. Climb 3 metres up a rope ladder or rope, or walk 6 metres over a rope bridge.

4. Go on foot for an expedition at least 6.5km long.

5. Meet a physical challenge set in consultation with your Guider and tester.

Part II

1. Knit or sew a simple garment.

2. 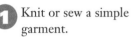Prepare, cook and serve a two-course meal on your own. Clear away and wash up afterwards.

3. Wash and iron a garment of your own.

4. Renew a tap washer.

Part III

1. Make a puppet or a soft toy.

2. Make a table decoration of flowers, twigs and/or leaves.

3. Sing four campfire songs, make your own musical instrument or tell a story.

4. Write a short poem or a sketch which takes at least six minutes to perform.

5. Use a program on a micro-computer.

Part IV

1. Light a fire out of doors and cook on it.

2. Know your neighbourhood well enough to be able to give clear directions to the tester.

3. Demonstrate the practical use of square lashing and four of these knots: clove hitch, round turn and two half hitches, sheetbend, timber hitch, donkey hitch, double overhand, fisherman's, packer's, reef.

4. Draw, photograph or describe at least 18 natural specimens which you have seen growing. Know something about them.

Part V

1. Hear or read two stories about people, places or events in the history of the Guide Movement.

2. Meet some members of the Movement who are not in your unit, and make a swap pin (badge) to give one of them.

3. Save up and buy a World Badge. Know what its symbols mean.

4. Pass a Be Prepared test arranged by the tester. This will include improvisation, dealing with a sudden emergency, coping with change of plans, unexpected situations and difficult or unusual jobs.

Date: 7/3/96

Tester's signature

T. Taylor

My signature

Liane Ireland

C

21

Stage 1

Note *If you hold the Preliminary Certificate of Merit of the British Chess Federation and complete Clause 5, you may have this badge.*

1 Set out a chess board ready for a game to be played.

2 Demonstrate the moves that each piece can make.

3 Know the rules of the game.

4 Understand the meaning of check and checkmate.

5 Observed by the tester, play a game with another player.

Stage 2

Note *If you hold the Intermediate Certificate of Merit of the British Chess Federation and complete Clause 4, you may have this badge.*

1 Complete Clauses 1 to 4 of Stage 1.

2 Be able to use the algebraic system of chess notation, recognised by the World Chess Federation.

3 Demonstrate the use of:

a castling

b taking procedure with pawns.

4 Observed by the tester, play a game with another player.

Stage 3

Note *If you hold the Higher Certificate of Merit of the British Chess Federation and complete Clause 5, you may have this badge.*

1 Complete Clauses 1 to 3 of Stage 2.

2 Understand and demonstrate the following basic patterns:

a the knight fork

b the pin

c the skewer.

3 Show checkmate positions on a chess board using:

a rooks

b bishops.

4 Demonstrate two openings to the tester.

5 Observed by the tester, play a game with another player.

Stage 4

Note *If you hold the Advanced Certificate of Merit of the British Chess Federation and complete Clause 5, you may have this badge.*

1 Complete Stage 3.

2 Demonstrate the following moves:

a king's gambit

b queen's gambit

c 'greek gift' checkmate attack from a position set up by the tester.

3 Be able to recognise a range of strategies that can be used in a game, and describe the moves which a player may make in order to win a game from three set end-game positions.

4 Analyse and comment on a written game set by the tester.

5 Observed by the tester, play a game against a player of your own standard or a higher one. (A time limit should be set by the tester.)

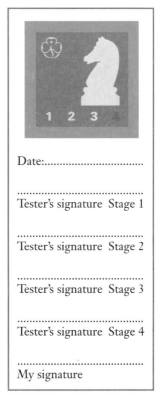

Date:................................

....
Tester's signature Stage 1

....
Tester's signature Stage 2

....
Tester's signature Stage 3

....
Tester's signature Stage 4

....
My signature

CHILD CARE

You must have a sense of responsibility and a high standard of personal cleanliness. You should understand that when dealing with a child you must carry out whatever you have said you will do, and should not resort to bribery. Remember to report any accident the child might have while in your care, particularly if it involves the head.

Notes

- *The syllabus refers throughout to children aged between three and five years old.*

- *You can take the test in two parts. If necessary a different tester can test Part II.*

Part I

1 Know how to clothe a child in summer and winter.

2 Know what sort of food she/he should eat.

3 Tell the tester what sorts of play materials are suitable for the child.

4 Plan a day's activities. Tell the tester why children respond to a regular routine.

5 Know how to prevent accidents indoors or in a garden.

6 Be able to treat simple cuts and bruises.

7 Know how to put a child to bed.

Part II

Take charge of a child or small group of children for part of a day supervised by the tester. You will be asked to:

a   Help to wash the child/children before a meal.

b   Serve a meal.

c   Set out suitable play material, and supervise its use, joining in if the child requires it.

d   Tell a story.

When you hold this badge you should be capable of taking charge of a child of the age group for any part of the day. However, you will not be expected to do so without an adult being within call.

Date..... 19/5/97 ....

.......Reland...............
Tester's signature

.....Liane Ireland..............
My signature

COLLECTOR   C

1 Over the period of at least six months make, or add to, a collection. Organise it and display it at the test.

Carry out some research into the subject of your collection. Perhaps you could read a book, visit a similar collection or talk to an expert.

c Tell the tester why you find your hobby interesting and some of the things you have learnt from it. Suggest ways in which you could develop your interest further.

2 Arrange for your Patrol to see your collection. Be able to talk about it and answer questions.

3 Visit a museum, art gallery, or other collection. Tell the tester about your visit, and describe the methods used to display the exhibits.

Date:..............................

....
Tester's signature

....
My signature

COMPUTER

Stage 1

1 Tell the tester about the computer(s)/printer(s), etc. with which you are familiar and say what each item is used for.

2 *Either*

Switch on a single computer, then load and run a program.

or

Use a computer connected to a network to log-on, select a program and run it.

3 Show how to type both small and capital letters and know where the space, enter (return), delete and function keys are.

4 Describe three uses of a computer in shops, factories, etc.

5 Keep a diary recording every time you use a computer for at least three months and take it with you to the test.

6 Learn how to play two new computer games, then explain to the tester how they are played, which you preferred and why.

Stage 2

1 Complete Clauses 1 to 3 of Stage 1.

2 Describe to the tester a task which can be done both manually and using a computer and explain the advantages and disadvantages of each method.

3 Choose two of the following and carry them out, using a computer, at the test:

a Use a word-processing package to produce a report of a Guiding event.

b Add, delete, amend and print records of a database.

c Use LOGO or a similar package to control a robot, turtle, etc. to follow a predetermined route.

d Use a graphics package to create a poster to publicise a Guiding event.

e Any other task of a similar level of difficulty.

Stage 3

1 Complete Clauses 1 to 3 of Stage 1.

2 Describe to the tester one use of computers and the economic, legal and moral effects it has had on employees, employers and society.

3 Choose three of the following and carry them out accurately, using a computer, at the test:

a Use a word-processing package to produce a multi-page report of a Guiding event which includes double-line spacing, underlining, centring, etc.

b Use a desktop publishing package to produce a leaflet which promotes Guiding.

c Create a database to hold information about members of your Unit e.g. name, current Journey or Trefoil Badge worn, Interest Badge held, and be able to amend, interrogate and print records. Please be aware of the Data Protection Act and the problems involved in creating a database with 'live' data, i.e. data on actual members of the Unit.

d Use a spreadsheet package to create next year's income and expenditure budgets for the Unit and investigate what happens if subs are increased.

e Use a graphics package to create a poster to recruit either girls or leaders into Guiding.

f Any other task of a similar level of difficulty.

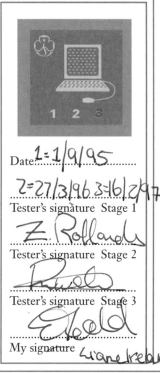

Date: 1 = 1/9/95

2 = 27/3/96 3 = 16/2/97

Tester's signature Stage 1

Z Rollands

Tester's signature Stage 2

Tester's signature Stage 3

My signature Diane Ireland

CONFECTIONER

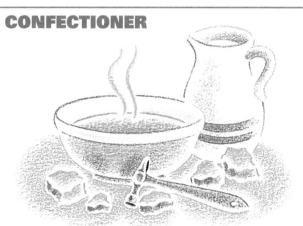

1 Know how to make three or more different icings. Tell the tester what each is suitable for.

2 Colour icing successfully.

3 At the test decorate:

a a cake suitable for a child's birthday party

b a small biscuit.

Use two different icings to do this and also show that you can use a piping bag and nozzle.

4 Bring to the test a selection of cooked and uncooked sweets which you have made. Present them attractively in a small container. Tell the tester how you made one of these sweets.

Date: 2/6/97

Tester's signature

S Baker

My signature Diane Ireland

CONSERVATION

1 Discuss with the tester the meaning of these words: ecology, conservation, energy.

Explain the differences between renewable and non-renewable energy sources. Find out about any recycling schemes in your area – collecting newspaper, aluminium, bottles and so on.

2 Choose an area such as part of a park, a churchyard, roadside verge or piece of waste ground. List all the plants you can find there and make a record of any evidence of animal life.

3 Do one of the following for four months. Discuss your plans with the tester before starting the clause and report to her after the four months.

a Cultivate a small parcel of land in a garden, churchyard, school or somewhere similar. Plant some British wild plants, or wild plants native to your country of residence.

b Join a group or society which works for conservation. Take part in one of their projects.

c Find out ways in which the average family wastes materials and other natural resources. Suggest how these can be conserved and put your suggestions into practice as far as possible. At the end of the four months decide how much has been saved.

Date:.............................

....
Tester's signature

....
My signature

COOKS

Stage 1

1 At the test make a snack e.g. egg on toast or a sandwich. Show skills that include the correct and safe use of equipment such as a chopping board, knives, etc.

2 Show your skill at preparing fresh fruit and vegetables.

3 Show your skill to prepare a healthy dish that requires little or no heat, e.g. fruit salad or salad.

4 Tell the tester what you understand by the term 'safety in the kitchen'.

5 Know how to wash up and clear away afterwards.

Stage 2

1 Prepare a series of dishes showing culinary skills. Your choice should take into account your culture. It should include two items from each of the following groups:

a milk, cheese, yoghurt, soya milk

b fresh fruit and vegetables

c breads, cereals, rice, oats or pasta

d egg, fish, cheese, meat, poultry, tofu, peas, beans or other pulses.

2 Make a recipe book of the recipes you have tried and indicate whether they are tasty.

3 At the test, make a meal for yourself and the tester using convenience foods.

Stage 3

1 Plan, cook and serve a two-course meal showing your competence in the following areas:

a method of cooking

b skills and safety in using a cooker/ microwave

c presentation, including garnishing, serving and correct table laying.

2 Understand what is meant by a healthy diet and plan a week's menu accordingly. For advice refer to your Section Handbook or File. You will also find that some supermarkets provide free leaflets on diet and nutrition.

3 Show your knowledge of good food hygiene practice when handling food, considering purchase, preparation and storage of food, and appropriate dress.

4 Using convenience foods create your own healthy dish at the test. Say which type of consumer would eat convenience foods.

Stage 4

1 Over a period of six months, keep a record of recipes you make at home, school or college. Show you have improved your skills and how you can adapt recipes to suit dietary needs. Dishes chosen should be recipes new to you, from magazines and other such resources.

Record your results – comment on how successful the dishes were and if they could be improved in any way. Comments could be from those who have eaten them.

2 Plan, cook and serve a meal for a group of people. Take a copy of the menu to the test and include planning and costings.

3 Take your favourite recipe to the test and show the tester how to make it. Explain why you have chosen it and its nutritional value.

Date:.....2/10/95.....

....
Tester's signature Stage 1

....
Tester's signature Stage 2

....
Tester's signature Stage 3

....
Tester's signature Stage 4

....
My signature

COUNTRY DANCE

> If you use a wheel-chair, either self-propelled or assisted, you may choose four dances, each one to be a different formation.

Notes

- *The dances named are given to show the standard expected. However, if you ask the tester's permission, you may substitute other dances of equal scope and difficulty.*

- *Choose one of the following sections and take part in the dances listed there. You can perform the dances in any position.*

England

Choose and perform two of these dances:

a Pins and Needles

b Cumberland Square Eight

c Nottingham Swing

d Waltz Country Dance.

Choose and perform two more dances of your own choice.

Wales

Hint A tape and instruction booklet is available from Guides Cymru (The Guide Association of Wales) Broneirion, Llandinam, Powys SY17 5DE.

Perform these two dances:

Ceiliog y Rhedyn

Difyrrwch Gwyr Dyfi

Choose and perform two dances from the following list:

a Wrth Fynd Efo Deio i Dywyn

b Ffaniglen

c Cambro Briton

d Lord of Caernarfon's Jig – Jig Arglwydd Caernarfon

27

e Oswestry Wake

f Y Jig Gymraeg

g Robin Ddiog.

Scotland

Hint The books listed below are published by the Royal Scottish Country Dance Society, 12 Coates Crescent, Edinburgh EH3 6AF.

Perform these dances:

a The Eightsome Reel as taught by the Royal Scottish Country Dance Society, *Book 2*

b River Cree, *Book 8*

c Fidget, *Book 16*

d *either*

Berwick Johnie, number 14 in the Graded Book and Mrs Macleod, *Book 6*

or

two more Scottish Country Dances of your own choice. If possible, one dance should have some local traditional interest.

Ulster

Perform two dances. These should be:

a Rincce Mor, Walls of Limerick or a solo reel and

b Bridge of Athlone, Harvestime Jig or Light Double Jig.

Choose and perform two more dances of your own choice.

Overseas Territories

Guides living overseas having chosen one of the above sections may substitute local dances.

Date:...........................

....
Tester's signature

....
My signature

CRAFT

Notes

- *You should have made only one of the items at school or college.*

- *One or more items must have been made in the last six months.*

- *One item must use a technique or skill new to you.*

- *If you make four more items you may have another Craft Badge.*

Do four of the following to make either a picture or a design, or to decorate an item of clothing or soft-furnishing, or to produce a three-dimensional piece of work.

a Embroidery (hand or machine).

b Tapestry.

c Fabric collage.

d Lace.

e 'Plastic canvas'.

f Produce a piece of weaving suitable to use as a table-mat, to make a small bag or purse, a floor covering, a decorative wall-hanging, or a belt.

g Spin some yarn from fleece on a simple hand spindle. Weave the yarn into a small piece of fabric.

h Carve a figure in any medium.

i Model a figure, or a group of animals.

j Make a pot. The piece may or may not be decorated: it can be glazed and fired.

k Make a mosaic design or picture.

l Make three prints, either decorative or pictorial using:

- potato print
- lino print
- polystyrene print
- string print
- etching
- drypoint
- aquatint
- screen print

or

- a combination of these methods.

The prints submitted should be a numbered series.

m Produce a piece of decorated fabric, or an item of clothing, or soft furnishing decorated using one (or more) of the following methods:

- block printing
- screen printing
- tie-dye
- direct painting.

n Produce a painting or a design on glass.

o Make an item, e.g. small bag, belt etc. using leather. Decorative methods can be used on the item, e.g. carving, embossing, studwork.

p Engrave a design or a picture on a glass object or a panel.

q Make a picture using the quilling technique.

r Decorate a wooden object, or produce a picture on a wooden panel using pyrography.

s Make (and dress if appropriate) a puppet.

t Make a basket.

u Calligraphy: write out a favourite poem, and a song of your own choice.

v Country crafts. Make a:

- corn-dolly
- flower-arrangement

or

- decorative candle for a festive occasion.

w Make an article using some other craft e.g. stained-glass, book binding.

Date: 2/6/96

....
Tester's signature

....
My signature

CRIME PREVENTION

① Obtain and read a leaflet on household security from your local police or an insurance company. Explain to the tester how a householder can make his or her house secure.

Explain how neighbours can help to protect your home from burglary. Find out how a Neighbourhood Watch scheme works.

② Know how car drivers can keep their parked cars and their contents secure.

③ In connection with callers at the door, explain:

a the use of a door viewer and a door chain

b why it might be dangerous for an elderly person to leave the door chain on all the time

c how you can make sure whether or not an official (such as a meter reader) or a salesman is genuine.

④ Tell the tester:

a what advice parents should give to children about talking to strangers

b what children must tell their parents when they are going out alone or with other children.

⑤ Design a poster to demonstrate any aspect of crime prevention.

⑥ Do the following:

a Explain the property marking schemes which use the post code.

b Know what is meant by visible and invisible marking and how they are achieved.

c Take to the test samples of property which are suitable for visible and invisible marking.

⑦ Tell the tester what a Crime Prevention

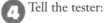

Panel is and what it tries to achieve. Suggest some projects that it could undertake.

8 Explain to the tester what personal safety precautions you should take:

a when walking alone along a street

b if approached by a stranger in a car

c if you think you are being followed.

Date:...........................

....
Tester's signature

....
My signature

CULTURE

Stage 1

1 Write down details of your own cultural background. These should include:

a your nationality

b the meaning of one of your names

c your faith or religion

d the flag of your country.

2 Visit a place of historical interest in the area in which you are living. If possible, make this visit with members of your Six, Patrol or Unit.

3 Know about a song, dance or craft which is from your own cultural background, or local to the area in which you are living.

4 Bring to the test a type of food which is traditional in your own culture or in the area in which you are living.

5 Talk to an adult known to you (other than a member of your own family), from your own culture, and find out about their lifestyle.

Stage 2

1 Find out where one or more of the adult members of your family group were born and talk to them about their lifestyle when they were your age (e.g. what they wore for school, casual wear, special occasions, about their home life, meal times, cooking, washing, hobbies, customs, festivals).

2 Know your own National Anthem and be able to sing it in your first language.

3 Find out about a well-known person connected with the locality in which you live, and find a book in your local library which refers to her or him.

4 Learn a song, dance or craft from your own cultural background or local to the community in which you are living.

5 Cook a dish which is traditional in your own culture or in the area in which you are living.

6 Talk to an adult known to you (other than a member of your own family group), from your own culture, about her or his faith. Find out what they believe and why.

Stage 3

1 Begin a record of your own family group.

2 Show in an interesting way (e.g. photographs, scrapbook, box of treasures or artefacts) the things which you think are important and show your cultural background. Before the test show this to your Six, Patrol or Unit.

3 Find out about the origin of the name of the village, district or town in which you are living. Discover how and why it developed as it did.

4 Teach your Six, Patrol or Unit a dance or craft from your own culture or locality, and tell them about its origin or meaning.

5 Cook a simple two-course meal using traditional food and/or recipes from your own culture or from the area in which you are living.

6 Talk to someone from a different cultural background and find out about their lifestyle

Stage 4

1 Make a record of your family group, going back as far as possible.

2 Make a book to give as a gift to an overseas friend. This should show as much as possible about you and your lifestyle, your local community and your country. This could be taken by you on a visit abroad, or given to someone to take back to their country, so watch the size and weight!

3 Tell a story or legend about your local community.

4 Make a leaflet or chart from which others could learn a dance or craft from your culture or locality.

5 Cook a simple two-course meal using food which is traditional to a culture different from your own and from the area in

which you are living. Try to eat the meal in a traditional way (e.g. for a Chinese or Japanese meal use chopsticks and sit or kneel in the traditional manner).

6 Talk to someone from a different faith and cultural background and find out what she or he believes and why.

Date:..............................

....
Tester's signature Stage 1

....
Tester's signature Stage 2

....
Tester's signature Stage 3

....
Tester's signature Stage 4

....
My signature

CYCLIST

The Royal Society for the Prevention of Accidents recommend wearing safety helmets.

Hint For a copy of the Code of Practice on Safe Cycling, please send a stamped addressed envelope to: Youth Activities, The Guide Association, 17–19 Buckingham Palace Road, London SW1W 0PT.

Stage 1

1 Own or part-own a bicycle of the appropriate size.

2 Keep your bicycle clean and know how to check it is in safe working order (if necessary, with adult help).

3 Know how to find out about lighting-up time. Know why lights and bright clothing are necessary when you are cycling.

4 Go with the tester for a ride showing that you can ride your bicycle safely (off-road), that you use the brakes correctly and that you understand:

a the rules of the road for cyclists

b the signals that cyclists give and observe

c the correct way to turn right into a side road.

Stage 2

1 a *Either*

Attend a training course and pass the National Cycling Proficiency Test

or

Equivalent test run by your local authority.

or

Ride your bicycle on a short route (on quiet roads) planned by the tester. Show that you can control your machine safely and confidently and be in the correct position on the highway. You must show you can start and stop safely. You will be asked to carry out left and right turns and an emergency stop. You should also know how cyclists use traffic lights, pedestrian crossings of all types, roundabouts and signed cycle routes in towns. Know how to park your bicycle safely.

b Demonstrate cycle control in a safe area (such as a playground) by riding in and out of a line of blocks or, preferably, cones.

2 **a** Demonstrate how to check your bicycle is safe to use on the road (especially brakes, tyres and chain). Know how to maintain your bicycle in good working order.

b Know how to adjust saddle and handlebars to correct height for your use.

3 Have a practical knowledge of the Highway Code as it relates to you as a cyclist and tell the tester about the dangers of dark or loose clothing, personal stereos, badly arranged loads, carrying passengers, and inadequate lighting when cycling at night or in poor visibility.

4 Bring to the test records of at least three cycle rides to places of interest, one of which will have been of at least six miles. If the routes include sections 'off-road' know the Off-road Cycling Code.

5 Make up a small first aid kit suitable for carrying on a cycle trip. Collect items for a simple tool and puncture repair kit. Bring both to the test and show a knowledge of the use of both.

Stage 3

1 Clauses 1, 2 and 5 of Stage 2 must be passed.

2 Be able to read an Ordnance Survey map of suitable scale for cycling. At the test plan a route between places suggested by the tester, taking into account traffic, terrain, etc. This can include 'off-road' sections if appropriate.

3 Keep a record of three rides to places of interest (one to be of at least 15 miles). The record should include details of prior planning, route taken and equipment carried. If routes are off-road, the Off-road Cycling Code must be observed.

4 Demonstrate at the test that you have a knowledge of suitable clothing for a cycle trip, taking into account your visibility to other road users, your personal safety and the weather conditions which may be encountered.

Stage 4

1 Pass Clause 1 of Stage 3.

2 Plan and lead two cycling tours of at least 30 miles for three or four cyclists, on- or off-road. Keep a logbook of the tours.

3 Discuss your plans with the tester beforehand. The tester will wish to be satisfied that your map reading, first aid and safety knowledge are adequate. (The permission of your parents/guardians must be obtained.)

4 Know the Off-road Cycling Code.

Date:...............................

....
Tester's signature Stage 1

....
Tester's signature Stage 2

....
Tester's signature Stage 3

....
Tester's signature Stage 4

....
My signature

DANCER

Note *You must tell the tester before the test which dance form you have chosen. The syllabus used should be acceptable to the Council for Dance Education and Training.*

1 Know one characteristic national dance from three different countries in any part of the world. Perform at least one of these three dances at the test, and demonstrate one or more steps from the others.

Tell the tester the historical background of the dances and something about the costumes worn when the dances are performed.

2 Using any dance form you choose:

a Perform a dance lasting about three minutes.

b *Either*
Improvise on your chosen dance form to music or some other form of which has been chosen by the tester.

or

Perform a set dance selected by the tester.

Date:..............................

....
Tester's signature

....
My signature

DEAF AWARENESS

Hint Contact the Royal National Institute for Deaf People (RNID). Look in the telephone book for the address of your nearest branch. The Head Office is at 105 Gower Street, London WC1E 6AH.

Stage 1

1 Learn the manual alphabet and use it to:

a tell the tester your name

b ask the tester her/his name and understand her/his reply.

2 Find out and tell the tester about hearing dogs and their uses.

3 Take part in a game or activity with your Unit while wearing earplugs or head phones, making you unable to hear clearly.

4 Show the tester the correct way to approach a deaf person and how to speak to her/him in order for that person to lip-read.

Stage 2

1 Using a sign language and, where necessary, the manual alphabet, show you can:

a introduce yourself to a deaf person and tell that person something about your home and a hobby you enjoy

b understand something the tester tells you about herself/himself.

Make sure you know how to say 'I don't understand'.

2 Know something about the work of one of the National Voluntary Organisations which serve the needs of deaf people and those with a hearing loss such as:

- Sense
- The National Deaf Children's Society
- Friends of the Young Deaf.

Share this information with members of your Unit.

3 Show the tester the symbol that indicates

which facilities have provision for people with a hearing impairment.

4 Know the importance of facial expression and gesture when you are communicating with a deaf person. Find out what it is like to be deaf or have a hearing loss by talking to someone with this disability, and tell the tester how this affects that person's life.

Stage 3

1 Be able to sign a simple story, poem or song and answer six questions signed to you, replying in sign language.

2 Find out something about a famous deaf person, e.g. Jack Ashley MP, Evelyn Glennie, Elizabeth Quinn, Beethoven, and tell the tester what you have learned.

3 What hazards or difficulties could a deaf person encounter in daily living and what safety devices are available to help e.g. fire alarms, minicom, etc?

4 Take part in a social event with one or more members of the deaf community e.g. at a club, school, or special unit, or by helping on a holiday or play scheme.

Stage 4

1 Using sign language hold a conversation on a chosen subject with a deaf person for at least ten minutes.

2 Find out about the development of hearing aids to the present day, e.g. ear trumpet, phonic ear, etc. Give a talk about them to a group of people.

3 Investigate the difficulties faced by someone with a hearing impairment who has an additional disability e.g. blindness and explain these difficulties to the tester.

4 Make up or adapt a game for a child with a hearing loss.

5 Complete one of the following:

a   Design something

which will enable a deaf person to become more independent.

b   Show the tester how you would teach road safety to a child with a hearing loss.

c   Show the tester how you would make a house safe for an elderly person with a hearing loss.

Date:...............................

....

Tester's signature Stage 1

Tester's signature Stage 2

Tester's signature Stage 3

Tester's signature Stage 4

....

My signature

DINGHY SAILOR

Note *The following abbreviations are used throughout this syllabus:*

- *IOCA*
  International Optimist Class Association

- *NSSA*
  National Schools Sailing Association

- *RYA*
  The Royal Yachting Association.

Stage 1

Notes

- *If you hold the RYA Young Sailors' Award Level 1, NSSA Bronze, IOCA Grade 1 or RYA National Dinghy Certificate Level 1 and complete Clause 1 below, you may have this badge.*

- *The tester should be a qualified instructor or an experienced sailor over the age of 16 whom the County Assistant Outdoor Activities Adviser (Boating) considers suitable. Clauses 1 and 12 may be tested by this person.*

1 Swim 50 metres and stay afloat for five minutes wearing clothes. This clause may be done in a swimming pool and you may wear a buoyancy aid if you wish.

2 Present yourself for the test in suitable clothing and put on a buoyancy aid correctly. Be able to explain why your clothing is suitable and why you wear a buoyancy aid.

3 Know the names of basic parts of a boat: hull, mast, rudder, tiller, centreboard.

4 Be aware of wind direction.

5 Assist with rigging a dinghy.

6 Launch a dinghy and get underway with assistance.

7 Demonstrate that you can steer and turn a dinghy in light winds and when being towed.

8 Know, and if possible demonstrate, how to stay with your boat in the event of capsize.

9 Assist with coming ashore, recovery and putting away of dinghy and sails.

10 Know how to call for assistance and how to prepare to be towed.

11 Show that you can paddle or row a dinghy round a short triangular course.

12 Tie and know when to use a figure-of-eight (stopper) knot.

Stage 2

Notes

● *If you hold the RYA Young Sailors' Award Stage 2, NSSA Silver IOCA Grade 2 or RYA National Dinghy Certificate Level 2 and complete Clause 1 below, you may have this badge.*

● *The tester for Clauses 2 to 10 should be an instructor or experienced sailor whom the County Assistant Outdoor Activities Adviser (Boating) considers suitable. This person may also test Clause 1.*

1 Swim 50 metres and stay afloat for five minutes wearing clothes. This clause may be done in a swimming pool and you may wear a buoyancy aid if you wish.

2 Present yourself for the test in suitable clothing and buoyancy aid. Be able to explain your choice of personal gear to the tester.

3 Know some ways of observing wind direction. Know what is meant by windward and leeward.

4 Rig a dinghy, with assistance if required.

5 Get underway from and return to a beach or pontoon in a light offshore wind.

6 Demonstrate in light winds under supervision:

  a sailing a set course across the wind

  b going about

  c getting out 'of irons'

  d stopping by lying wind abeam

  e awareness of other water users and a basic understanding of the 'rules of the road'.

7 Crew a dinghy effectively showing adjustment of jib, centreboard and body weight.

8 *Either*

Show how to capsize and right a single-handed dinghy.

or

Show how to be scooped in during recovery of a capsized dinghy.

9 Know how to prepare for a multiple tow.

10 Know how to tie and use a round turn and two half hitches, bowline and figure-of-eight (stopper) knot.

Stage 3

Notes

● *If you hold the RYA Young Sailors' Award Stage 3 or RYA National Dinghy Certificate Level 2 and complete Clauses 1 and 10*

below, you may have this badge.

• *The tester for Clauses 2 to 8 should be an RYA Instructor or hold a qualification approved by the County Assistant Outdoor Activities Assistant (Boating). This person may also test Clauses 1, 9 and 10.*

1 Swim 50 metres and stay afloat for five minutes wearing clothes. This clause may be done in a swimming pool and you may wear a buoyancy aid if you wish.

2 Present yourself suitably dressed for the test and discuss your choice of clothing and buoyancy aid. Know how to check your boat is safe

before going afloat.

3 Rig and launch a dinghy. Either demonstrate or show that you understand:

a how to launch in an onshore wind

b how to sail backwards from a pontoon in an offshore wind.

4 Understand how to adjust rigging to suit the weather conditions. Reef a dinghy ashore.

5 Demonstrate that you can:

a tack proficiently

b gybe proficiently

c sail on a beat, reach and run

d apply the 'five essentials' (sail setting, balance, trim, centreboard, course made good)

e recover a 'man overboard'

f stop the boat

g return to shore, mooring or jetty safely.

6 Know the basic 'rules of the road' (port/starboard, windward boat and overtaking boat) and any particular conditions or hazards in the area in which you usually sail. Explain what precautions you would take before going afloat and where to obtain a weather forecast.

7 Know what action to take when in distress and how to help others in distress.

8 *Either*

Show how to capsize and right a single-handed dinghy.

or

Show how to capsize a dinghy and be scooped in during recovery.

9 Tie and know when to use: a figure-of-eight (stopper), round turn and two half hitches, bowline and reef.

10 Know how to recognise and deal with hypothermia. Describe to the tester how you would deal with cuts, a

bang on the head, blisters and rope burn. Demonstrate artificial respiration using a manikin.

Stage 4

Notes

• *If you hold the RYA Young Sailors' Scheme Advanced Sailing White Award or the RYA National Dinghy Scheme Level 3 and complete Clause 1 below, you may have this badge.*

• *The tester for Clauses 2 to 15 should be an RYA Instructor or hold a qualification approved by the County Assistant Outdoor Activities Adviser (Boating). This person may also test Clauses 1 and 16.*

1 Swim 50 metres and stay afloat for five minutes wearing clothes. This clause may be done in a swimming pool and you may wear a buoyancy aid if you wish.

2 Present yourself for the test wearing suitable clothing and a buoyancy aid. Be able to describe the standards used to grade buoyancy aids and what personal gear is suitable for different conditions.

3 Know what safety measures to take before going afloat and what equipment to take with you.

4 Rig and launch a dinghy to suit the weather conditions.

5 Leave and return to shore, jetty or mooring. Know, and if possible demonstrate, how to do this from both windward and leeward shores.

6 Sail to best advantage round a given course showing an understanding of balance, trim, centreboard, set of sails on different points of sailing, and course made good. Know and apply basic 'rules of the road'.

7 Demonstrate that you can:

  a come alongside a moored boat

  b sail in close company with other boats

  c be towed

  d tow another sailing dinghy

  e heave to

  f recover a 'man overboard'

  g reef afloat.

8 Know the principles of anchoring. Demonstrate that you can use and stow an anchor.

9 Know about buoyancy bags/tanks and how the distribution of buoyancy affects the capsized dinghy.

10 Demonstrate how to right a capsized dinghy, bail out and sail on.

11 Paddle and row a dinghy round a short triangular course.

12 Know the names for the parts of a boat and sails, the terms for position relative to the boat and for boat manoeuvres.

13 Tie and know when to use these knots: figure-of-eight (stopper), round turn and two half hitches, sheetbend, clove hitch, rolling hitch, bowline and fisherman's bend. Demonstrate common whipping, heat sealing and eye splice.

14 Know why you need to be aware of the weather and how to obtain weather forecasts and information. Know the characteristics of high and low pressure areas, the significance of changes in barometric pressure and the Beaufort scale. Give a *simple* interpretation of a synoptic chart.

15 Know the hazards and features of the waters you normally sail. If this is tidal water, be able to explain how to predict tides, the rule of twelfths, and the effect of wind, tide and current. Show that you can use the local tide tables.

16 Know how to recognise and deal with hypothermia.

Demonstrate:

  a how to stop bleeding

  b how to identify and treat a broken bone

  c how to treat an unconscious breathing patient.

Demonstrate how to give expired air resuscitation using a manikin.

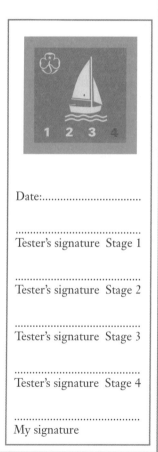

Date:................................

....
Tester's signature Stage 1

....
Tester's signature Stage 2

....
Tester's signature Stage 3

....
Tester's signature Stage 4

....
My signature

DOWNHILL SKIER

Disabled skiers may use any necessary extra equipment, e.g. outriggers.

Note *For alternative European qualifications please contact: Youth Activities, The Guide Association, 17-19 Buckingham Palace Road, London SW1W 0PT.*

Stage 1

Disabled skiers who cannot fulfil any of the requirements for Clauses 1 and 2 may demonstrate a controlled descent, turning and stopping instead.

Note *This badge may be awarded if you hold the British Alpine Ski Award Two Star Award and pass Clauses 1b, 4c and d.*

1 Demonstrate the following:

a carrying skis

b turning around in a limited space, using a kick turn or step turn

c side-stepping up and turning on the slope

d a snowplough for controlled descent, at a slow speed, with ability to stop at any moment

e downhill traversing to the right and to the left

f getting up on a slope after a fall.

2 Make four linked snowplough turns.

3 Do a straight schuss without falling.

4 Understand:

a the principles of release bindings

b the adjustment of the bindings in use

c the principle of ski brakes, and the reason they are used

d the correct fit of a ski boot.

5 Show or describe suitable clothing and equipment for skiing on the following slopes:

a artificial

b snow in all weather conditions.

6 Know the safety rules that apply to skiing on either artificial slopes or snow slopes. Explain the procedure in the event of an accident.

Stage 2

Note *Stage 2 of this badge may be awarded if you hold the British Alpine Ski Award Three Star Award and pass Clauses 1d and 4.*

1 Demonstrate the following:

a sideslipping (both sides)

b swinging to the hill from a steep traverse (both sides)

c rhythmically linked stem christies.

2 Make a controlled descent of at least 150 metres, showing consideration to other skiers.

3 Make several successful ascents of either a ski tow (drag lift) or a chairlift (using skis).

4 Know the symptoms of exposure and methods of treatment.

Stage 3

Note *Stage 3 of this badge may be awarded if you hold the British Alpine Ski Award Four Star Award and pass Clause 1.*

1 You must have skied on more than one slope.

2 Demonstrate at least ten long radius parallel turns with good leg extension.

3 Ski in control over bumps, absorbing them with your legs.

4 Make a controlled descent of a red run, showing consideration for other skiers.

5 Choose the route on easier terrain, showing sensible choice of line and good awareness of hazards.

6 Explain the dangers of a mountain environment.

Stage 4

Note *Stage 4 of this badge may be awarded if you hold the British Alpine Ski Award Five Star Award.*

1 Demonstrate the following on snow:

a at least ten short swings, showing control of speed, rhythm and co-ordination

b at least ten parallel step turns

c at least ten parallel skate turns

d a terrain jump without a fall on landing.

2 Choose a good route down a red run and ski down it without falling. Vary your techniques to suit the terrain.

3 Be able to demonstrate sound posture and the effective use of skis.

4 Know how to select skis, prepare and maintain them.

5 Be able to find your way over a route using a resort map.

Date:................................

....
Tester's signature Stage 1

....
Tester's signature Stage 2

....
Tester's signature Stage 3

....
Tester's signature Stage 4

....
My signature

EMERGENCY HELPER (BIENNIAL)

Part 1 First Aid

 ❶

a Using a manikin or mask, demonstrate artificial ventilation by the mouth-to-mouth or mouth-to-nose method. Show how to place the patient in the recovery position in case he or she should vomit.

b Know how to use artificial ventilation and external chest compression, and in what circumstances, for example drowning, electrical accidents and smoke-filled rooms.

❷

a Know the signs and symptoms you would look for in the case of a fractured spine.

b Understand the danger of moving or handling a patient

when the extent of the injury is not known.

3 Show how to give first-aid treatment:

a to an unconscious person

b for severe bleeding

c for burns and scalds.

4 Assemble a small first-aid kit and show how you would use the contents.

5

a Know how to make an emergency phone call.

b Pass a message accurately by phone.

c Complete a list of useful telephone numbers.

6 Know what action to take when a person has swallowed a poisonous substance.

Part 2 In the House

7 Know how to deal with:

a clothing that catches fire

b a pan of fat that catches fire

c a fire caused by an oil stove or electric fire.

8 Following the necessary safety precautions be able to:

a Show that you know how to use portable gas stoves.

b Repair fuses (both cartridge and fuse wire types) and wire up a plug correctly.

c Be able to hammer a nail in straight and put a screw into wood.

d Turn off the main utilities in case of an emergency, i.e. gas, water and electricity.

e Under the supervision of her/his parent or other adult look after a small child for about an hour and keep the child happy, using simple available material.

f Know what to pack for a member of the family suddenly admitted to hospital.

Part 3 Out of Doors

9 Demonstrate your ability to read a street map and/or Ordnance Survey map and give clear directions.

10 Be able to do three of the following:

a Know what to do if lost in a wood, fog or town. Be able to help someone younger than yourself who is lost in a shop or in the street.

b Recognise four poisonous plants or berries. Know what to do if anyone is found to have eaten any of these.

c Know the common causes of fire in the countryside and know what to do if you discover a fire including forest, moorland, heath and standing crops.

d Bring a note from an adult to say that with two friends you have cooked a hot meal in adverse conditions using wood gathered nearby.

Date:..............................

....
Tester's signature

....
My signature

ENGLISH FOLK

1 Explain the composition of the flag of St George and tell his story.

2 Make an interesting presentation (display, scrapbook, talk) on one of the following:

a a local/national tradition e.g. York/Lincoln mystery plays, wassailing/mummers' play, Guy Fawke's night, Olney pancake race

b the origins of such dishes as Bath Oliver biscuits, Richmond maid of honour.

3 *Either*
Take part in a Morris dance or other folk dance such as Cumberland Square Eight or Maypole dancing or the Playford selection.

or

Read and talk to your tester about Chaucer's Canterbury Tales

or

Tell a legend from your local area e.g. the Lambton Worm, Byardi Lear, Peg O'Nell etc.

or

Sing a folk song from your own area.

4 Explain the meaning of ten English place names. Choose them from different counties.

5

a Learn one of the following crafts: corn dollies, Dorset buttons, rag rug making, crazy patchwork, Somerset patchwork, barge painting, Durham quilting, basket making or pillow lace.

b Make one of the following and take to the test: Eccles cakes, Shrewsbury biscuits, Bakewell pudding, Chelsea buns, Everton toffee, Grantham gingerbreads, Cornish pasties or Lincolnshire 'n' Melton Mowbray pork pie.

Date:...............................

....
Tester's signature

....
My signature

ENTERTAINER **e**

1 Give a performance, lasting not less than four minutes, including one or more of the following: dancing, singing, playing an instrument, reciting, miming, and telling a story.

2 Either alone or with members of your Patrol, entertain others for at least ten minutes in one or more of the following ways:

a giving a puppet play

b dramatising a story or ballad

c making a shadowgraph

d taking part in a concert or play

e performing an item of your own choice.

Practise this clause so that your standard is high enough for a public entertainment and send a programme to the tester beforehand.

Date: 10/7/97

....
Tester's signature

G.Galbraith

My signature *Diane Ireland*

FAITH AWARENESS

Notes

● *Each of the four staged badges should be taken with the support of a member of the worshipping community to which you belong or where you would like to start your quest for faith. Stage 1 is for you if you have no experience of a worshipping community. If you already attend classes organised by your place of worship, you will want to start at one of the later stages. Every clause is designed for you – you must fit it into your pattern of worship, your talents and abilities, and your interests. The adult helping you will want to be sure you have found out more about the faith of your choice than you knew when you started the badge and that you have strengthened your understanding of the Promise. Don't forget to show this syllabus to her/him.*

● *If you wish to have a copy of this syllabus in another language or have any queries concerning the syllabus, please contact: The Development Officer, Guiding Services,*

The Guide Association, 17-19 Buckingham Palace Road, London, SW1W 0PT.

Stage 1

1 Attend your place of worship regularly.

2 Take part in an act of worship in your Unit.

3 Show members of your Unit an item or ritual used in your place of worship.

4 Draw, or make a collage or a model, of a religious celebration.

5 Talk to your Guider about a good turn you have done for your worshipping community and explain how it has helped you understand your Promise.

Stage 2

1 Attend your place of worship regularly. Draw a plan or picture or take a photograph of your place of worship. Show this to a leader of your worshipping community and find out if she/he knows any interesting stories about it.

2 With your Six, Patrol or Unit help to plan and carry out an act of worship in your Unit using mime, reading, music, dance, etc.

3 Read a book, watch a video or hear a story about someone whose faith plays an important part in her/his life. Talk to an adult leader about your chosen person, who may be someone in the past or present.

4 Find out about the meaning of a religious festival of your own faith. Tell your Six, Patrol or Unit about what you have learned.

5 Find out about an organisation which is working for the good of others. Use your findings to help others understand the purpose of the organisation.

6 Choose or write a prayer about keeping the Promise and use it at a suitable occasion.

Stage 3

1 Attend your place of worship regularly.

Undertake a responsibility in some activity of your worshipping community.

2 Enable a group of young people to plan and carry out an act of worship.

3 Find six passages in your holy book which relate to current everyday situations. Explain (to an adult) why you chose them.

4 *Either*

Find out about the beliefs of at least two faiths or denominations different from your own.

or

Find out all you can about other opportunities for worship in your area.

5 Find out about the needs of a disadvantaged group in your local community. Find out how you and/or your Unit can be of service to them. Plan with others how to carry out this service.

6 Explain the meaning of the Promise to another member of The Guide Association. Choose or write

a prayer within your faith which helps understanding of the Promise.

Stage 4

1 Attend your place of worship regularly and undertake a responsibility within your worshipping community.

2 Oversee the planning of worship in your Unit for a term, ensuring that individual members and groups have the opportunity to plan and participate.

3 Study your holy book or sacred writings and be able to suggest suitable readings for two themes, such as peace, thanksgiving, forgiveness, our world, our community, etc. Find or compose prayers to fit the themes you choose and use them at a suitable occasion.

4 Know the places and patterns of worship in your area and be able to direct others to them.

5 Become involved with a project supported by your worshipping community.

6 Find a different Promise from each of the four World Regions. Discuss with your Commissioner the differences and what your own Promise means to you.

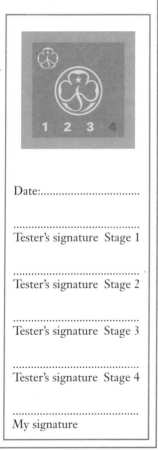

Date:...............................

....
Tester's signature Stage 1

....
Tester's signature Stage 2

....
Tester's signature Stage 3

....
Tester's signature Stage 4

....
My signature

f FARMER

When you go to the test, you must take a letter from your parents, a farmer or other responsible person with whom you have worked, to show your interest in the subject. The letter must state that you are aware of all the safety requirements when working on or visiting a farm or other agricultural establishment.

Note *This badge is divided into different parts. Choose the part that you wish to do and complete all the necessary clauses to gain your badge. If you complete another part you may gain and wear another Farmer Badge.*

Farm Worker

Please note the word 'farm' includes croft, market garden, smallholding, city farm or children's farm for the purposes of this badge.

1 Spend at least eight days (not necessarily consecutively) on a farm, helping as much as possible. Keep a record of what you do.

2 For a further eight days (not necessarily consecutively or on the same farm), under the supervision of the farmer/stock keeper, assist in one of the following options:

Either

a Look after, feed and keep clean one of the following: calves, pigs, a goat, a stabled pony, sheep or comparable livestock.

or

b Carry out work connected with the crop production of one of the following: cereals or grass, root crops including potatoes, soft or top fruit, hops, flowers or comparable crops.

3 Select a piece of equipment which was essential to the work you did in Clause 2; using the equipment itself or diagrams, photographs etc. show the tester how it is used, why it is essential to the job, and how it is maintained.

4 Discover what major types of farming are practised in the United Kingdom and plot them on a map of the UK. Be able to explain how the relief of the land and the amount of rainfall might influence the type of farming in an area.

Dairy

If you take this part, you must be aware of the safe practice for every clause you do.

1 Prepare a cow or goat for milking and demonstrate your ability to milk by hand or machine, as appropriate. The preparation should include washing and drying the teats and udder and drawing the foremilk into a suitable container. Have a basic knowledge of feeding and foodstuffs, including the different types of food which are fed for maintenance and production.

2 Be able to put the milk through the correct treatment, using the filter and cooling equipment, in the farm dairy. You may use bulk tanks if you wish.

3 Have a basic knowledge of the action of a milking machine, for example, vacuum and pulsation.

4 Wash and sterilise all the equipment.

5 Know why you clean and sterilise.

6 Help regularly for four weeks or more with a dairy routine in a cowshed or parlour or with goats. During this time keep suitable records showing, for example, the decline in milk yield through drying off, the effect of any illness or stress or the increase of milk yield after calving or kidding.

Rabbit Keeper

If you take this part, you must be aware of the safe practice for every clause you do.

Note *Your test should be spread over six months, so that the tester can inspect the rabbits and their accommodation from time to time.*

1 Keep rabbits for one year. Rear a litter and keep records showing their breeding, food and weights. Know the right way to handle rabbits.

2 Recognise the difference between fur, fancy and utility breeds. Know their uses.

3 Describe the common rabbit ailments such as scours, cold in the eye, and pot belly. Understand how to prevent and cure them.

4 Write diet sheets for one rabbit during the summer and winter. Recognise common plants which are suitable and those which are unsuitable for feeding rabbits.

Poultry Keeper

If you take this part you must be aware of the safe practice for every clause you do.

Note *Your test should be spread over three months so that the tester can inspect the poultry and their accommodation from time to time.*

1 Look after poultry regularly for at least six months or two school terms. If possible there should be at least six laying hens, ducks or geese. While you are looking after the poultry, keep a record of egg production and the cost of food and other items.

2 Set a hen, or set up a brooder. Rear chicks, ducklings or turkeys.

3 Know the difference between light hybrids and medium hybrids.

4 Understand why cleanliness is so important. Know why poultry houses should be disinfected and fresh water supplied.

Understand the elements of feeding poultry and the use of simple drugs to prevent diseases.

5 Pass one of the following:

a Clean out and disinfect the inside of a poultry house. Creosote the outside of it.

b Help to build a fowl house.

c Make a hen coop or run.

d Pluck and dress a bird for the table.

Bee Keeper

If you take this part, you must be aware of the safe practice for every clause you do.

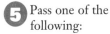

1 Understand why protective clothing is necessary when dealing with bees. Know how to deal with bee stings, including what to do in case of an allergic reaction.

2 Be responsible, or work closely with the person responsible, for keeping a hive of bees from March to October. Keep a record of the work you do.

3 Show that you can open up a hive of bees.

4 Identify the queen, drone and worker bees and their cells.

5 Assemble a frame and insert foundation.

6 Know the signs that indicate that the bees are preparing to swarm. Know what action to take.

7 Understand the principles of honey storage in the hive. Know the use of the queen excluder and supers.

8 Help with extracting honey and making up syrup for autumn feeding.

9 Know the basic principles of pollination and how pollen is collected by honey bees. From your own observation, name the flowers most frequently visited by the bees you are tending.

Date:................................

....
Tester's signature

....
My signature

FIREFIGHTER

Notes

- *If you complete the National Youth Firemanship Basic Course satisfactorily and pass Clause 7 you may have your Firefighter badge.*

- *Clause 1 may be covered by inviting a member of the local fire service to a meeting if this badge is not taken following a course at a fire station.*

1 Find out about the fire service in your area: appliances and equipment used, basic drills, and what happens when an emergency call comes in to the station. If you visit a station, know how to conduct yourselves throughout the visit.

2 Know the common causes of fires and cause of fire spread and basic precautions to be taken to prevent spread.

3 Know how to raise the alarm in the event of a fire, warning occupants if necessary, phoning the fire brigade using the emergency 999 system. Know the routing of the call and if possible visit your county control. Know the subsequent actions to be taken (basic precautions). Be aware of the use of a basic fire plan in your home.

4 Know how to deal with a fire indoors (chip pan/oil heater). Know what to do if a person's clothes are on fire. Know how to deal with grass or bushes on fire. Demonstrate how to crawl to safety from a smoke-filled room.

5 Be able to explain why smoke detectors are essential in the home and where they should be sited.

6 Be able to recognise the different kinds of extinguisher found in public places and know how to operate them.

7

a   Know how to deal with burns and shock.

b   Using a manikin or mask, demonstrate artificial ventilation by the mouth-to-

mouth or mouth-to-nose method. Show how to place the patient in the recovery position, in case she/he should vomit.

c Know when and how to use artificial ventilation and external chest compression, e.g. drowning, electrical accidents and smoke-filled rooms.

d Know the signs and symptoms you would look for in the case of a fractured spine.

e Understand the danger of moving or handling a patient when the extent of the injury is not known.

Date:..............................

....
Tester's signature

....
My signature

FIRST AID (BIENNIAL)

Notes

• *If you hold one of these certificates you qualify for this badge: British Red Cross Society Youth First Aid, St John Ambulance Association Essentials of First Aid or St Andrew's Ambulance Association Junior First Aid Certificate.*

• *The tester must be a qualified doctor, Registered Nurse on the UKCC register or the holder of any nationally validated adult First Aid Certificate approved by the District Commissioner.*

1

a Using a manikin or mask, demonstrate artificial ventilation by the mouth-to-mouth or mouth-to-nose method. Show how to place the patient in the recovery position in case he or she should vomit.

b Know how to use artificial ventilation and external chest compression, and in what circumstances, for example drowning, electrical accidents and smoke-filled rooms.

a Know the signs and symptoms you would look for in the case of a fractured spine.

b Understand the danger of moving or handling a patient when the extent of the injury is not known.

3 Have a basic understanding of the circulation. Show how to:

a stop bleeding

b dress a wound.

4 Know how and be able to manage an unconscious person after an accident, fit, fainting or other causes.

5 Know how to guard against shock following an accident.

6 Show how to prevent and deal with hypothermia.

7 Demonstrate the first-aid treatment for

f

burns, including those caused by acid or friction and scalds.

8 Bandage an injured ankle.

9 Know what to do if you suspect that someone has swallowed a poisonous substance.

10 Show how to use the telephone to summon help and deliver a clear message.

11 Know how to deal with a foreign body in the eye, ear, nose or throat.

12 Fit up a simple first-aid kit and know how to use the contents.

Date:...............................

....
Tester's signature

....
My signature

FITNESS

1 Show by your personal appearance at the test that you are genuinely interested in good health and grooming. Answer questions that the tester might ask you on the cleanliness of clothing and toilet articles, and the use and abuse of cosmetics and deodorants.

2 Show the efforts you are making to maintain good healthy habits by undertaking health challenges set by your Guider and/or your parents in the two months before the test.

3 Know why ill-fitting and unsuitable footwear is dangerous. Bring two pairs of your own shoes to the test. Tell the tester why you consider them suitable for different occasions such as going to school, to work, camping or to parties.

4 Describe the ways in which you try to keep your teeth and gums healthy.

5 Discuss with the tester how health is affected by cleanliness, smoking, food, alcohol, unwise dieting, drugs, deportment, exercise and late nights.

6 Discuss with the tester how you spend your leisure time. She/he will want to know if you are trying to maintain a balance in your various activities, interests and work.

Date:...............................

....
Tester's signature

....
My signature

FLOWER ARRANGER

1 Discuss with the tester:

a how to prepare flowers and leaves for a flower arrangement

b two methods of preserving leaves for winter decorations

c various methods of fixing flowers in a container

d how the law affects gathering wild flowers or plants.

2 At the test make two of the following arrangements:

a using an improvised or home-made container

b using wild plant materials

c using three flowers and any foliage

d an all-round display to be used as a table centre-piece

e a petite arrangement (under 23cm high).

Date:..............................

....
Tester's signature

....
My signature

FORESTER

1 Do the following:

a Mark on a sketch map places where 15 different species of trees grow. Identify their twigs, flowers, fruit and leaves.

b Make leaf prints or bark rubbings of three of the trees.

c Know what the wood from six of them can be used for.

2 Pot up and watch the development of six young seedlings, or successfully grow three from seed. Before your test, find out where and when these trees should be planted.

3 Show that you can use an axe or saw. Know how to look after them.

4 Visit a forest, arboretum, botanical gardens or saw mill. Tell the tester what interesting things you discovered there.

5 Know something about the care of trees, including pruning and thinning. Know how forest and woodland fires might be prevented.

Date:..............................

....
Tester's signature

....
My signature

FRIEND TO ANIMALS

For your safety, you should think carefully about the animal you choose and discuss the safety aspect with your Guider. This should be considered at each stage.

Note *For the purpose of this badge, animal may mean amphibian, bird, fish, insect, mammal or reptile.*

Stage 1

1 With the owners' permission get to know several different kinds of pets. Decide which would be right for you and which would be best for an old person living alone.

2 *Either*

If an animal already lives in your house, explain to the tester how you attempt to care for it.

or

If you do not yet have a pet, check out your house

f to see if you could give it what it needs.

You need to think about:

a how much space it needs

b the amount of exercise it needs

c type and cost of food

d how to keep it clean

e how much company it needs.

3 Find out about the best conditions for keeping two of the following animals happy and healthy:

a cat

b dog

c rabbit or guinea pig

d hamster, mouse or gerbil

e goldfish, cold-water or tropical fish

f stick insect, canary, budgerigar or parrot.

You can show the tester in any way you choose.

Stage 2

1 Take a full share in looking after your pet or another animal for at least three months. The animal might belong to someone else, for example, you might help look after an older person's dog, or it could be a classroom animal.

2 Arrange for the tester to meet your animal and tell her/him how you look after it. Do not forget to mention anything special it does.

3 Know what to do if you find a stray animal or lose your own animal.

4 Explain to the tester the differences between the work of the following:

a PDSA or Blue Cross

b RSPCA

c a veterinary surgeon.

5 Know the obedience training for your pet where appropriate.

Stage 3

1 For three months or more look after an animal suitable for keeping as a pet.

2 Know the causes and treatment of two common diseases or two reasons why your animal could be unwell.

3 Visit an animal or bird sanctuary, refuge, reserve or somewhere similar. Describe to the tester what you have learned about the care of animals or birds there.

4 Understand that close contact with some animals can pose health hazards for some people. Find out and discuss with the tester two possible health problems and how these could be avoided.

5 Pet owners have responsibilities. Discuss with the tester topics such as:

a noise and nuisance

b obedience training

c local bye-laws relating to animals.

Stage 4

1 Take full responsibility (for at least three months) for an animal suitable for keeping as a pet.

2 Understand, and be able to explain to a younger person, how and why breeding is controlled in your selected animal.

3 Explore the possibilities of showing your selected animal. This should include the breed standards and any special requirements. Visit a show and note what arrangements are made to prevent the animals suffering, for example from heat or lack of water, during the show.

4 Using any interesting method tell the story of St Francis, or an equivalent story in another religion, to a group of younger people.

5 Explain to a younger person why a working animal does not often make a suitable pet.

Date:...............................

....
Tester's signature Stage 1

....
Tester's signature Stage 2

....
Tester's signature Stage 3

....
Tester's signature Stage 4

....
My signature

GARDENER

1 Cultivate, keep tidy and crop a piece of ground, raised bed or window box for at least six months, preferably from March to September.

2 Know what type of soil you have, its advantages and disadvantages and how you can improve it. Know some of the reasons for applying organic manure and for using artificial fertilisers on your plot. Know which manure or fertiliser would benefit which crops.

3 Grow three different annual flowering plants and three different vegetables.

4 Know how to protect plants from the effects of drought, wind, frost and pests. Know which birds and beasts are beneficial to your plants and which ones are troublesome.

5 Show how to sow seeds, prune, take various types of cuttings and transplant a plant.

Know how to use and care for a spade, hoe and rake.

6 Know:

a The correct clothes to wear when gardening.

b The dangers involved when using insecticides and pesticides.

c The possible dangers when using electrical equipment in a garden. Discuss with the tester at least one type of safety device, such as guards, safety switches, circuit breaker plugs.

d How to deal with minor injuries such as cuts, splinters and scratches.

The test should be spread over a period of three months, during which the tester may wish to look at your plot from time to time.

Date:............................

....
Tester's signature

....
My signature

HANDYWOMAN

> Be careful when using any tool with sharp edges, surfaces etc.
>
> You may use electrical appliances if you have had adequate training or are being supervised by an adult.

1 Know where, in your own home, to turn off main supply of electricity, gas, oil, water (as connected).

2 Thoroughly clean, prepare and then repaint one of the following: chair, table, door, window frame or similar. Don't forget to clean your paint brushes and your hands thoroughly!

3 Show that you know how to use three common tools (not power-operated ones) for example, a hammer, pliers, saw, screwdriver, spanner etc.

4 Do six of the following:

a sharpen a knife

b fit a new handle to a handbag, shopping bag or equivalent

c fit a curtain rail and hang curtains

d lay vinyl overlay or floor tiles

e repair a mat or small carpet, or bind a carpet edge

f unblock a sink waste-pipe

g renew a tap washer

h repair a fuse with a cartridge or a fuse wire and know what precautions to take

i wire up an electric plug correctly and know what precautions to take

j cover a table, shelves or equivalent with adhesive plastic material

k lag pipes and a tank, and know what other precautions to take against burst pipes

l paint or colour-wash a ceiling or walls

m make something useful, an article for the house or garden, showing that you know how to use screws and nails correctly.

Date:.............................

....
Tester's signature

....
My signature

HERITAGE

1 Select one of the ancient kingdoms of the British Isles. With the help of your Patrol, and in any way you choose, show the tester what you have discovered about this ancient kingdom. You should include its:

a language and/or dialect

b folklore and legends

c music, songs and dances

d customs, ceremonies and dress

e family names or place names.

Be able to show on a map its boundaries and present-day counties and say how much of what you have discovered we have inherited today.

2 Do one of the following:

a Make a collection of commemorative stamps which you feel are representative of our heritage.

Find out about its origins and sketch or make models of the ceremonial clothes worn by some of the participants.

d Visit a 'living museum' or go on a heritage trail.

3 The badge design is Stonehenge and a tree. Be able to explain to a visitor from another country what Stonehenge is all about and why it is a World Heritage Site. The tester may impersonate the visitor.

The oak and the yew have a significant part in our heritage. Can you explain something about their importance?

4 *Either*

Discover which societies and groups in your town or county work together to carry out improvements, inaugurate new conservation projects or increase public knowledge of our heritage. Make a directory of these groups with notes on the work of their current projects.

b Collect traditional recipes from the United Kingdom and display them attractively, perhaps in a book or on cards.

c Either watch on TV/video or attend one of the following:

- Trooping the Colour
- State Opening of Parliament
- Ceremony of the Keys
- Swan Upping
- Service of Remembrance at the Cenotaph.

or

Study the national and local papers for a month, noting what efforts are being made to care for our heritage. Make a scrapbook of relevant press cuttings.

5 Know something of the history of The Guide Association and its place in the World Association of Girl Guides and Girl Scouts. Give a talk, set up an exhibition or play a game to share your knowledge with your Patrol.

HOBBIES

1 Show a continuing interest in your chosen hobby for at least three months.

2 Demonstrate to the tester how you pursue your hobby and what equipment, materials and background information you have used.

3 Discuss with the tester how you plan to develop your hobby or skill in the future.

Date:..............................

....
Tester's signature

....
My signature

Date: 24/9/96..........

....
Tester's signature

....
My signature
Liane

53

HOLIDAY

Note *This badge must be tested by someone holding a Holiday Licence or Camper's Licence.*

Take part in a Guide Holiday of at least two consecutive nights – this may be a Youth Hostelling trip.

1 Bring to the test a letter from the Guider in Charge of the holiday saying that you have:

a Taken part in the planning of the holiday. This would include deciding on the theme, programme and menus and finding out about places of interest near the holiday home/youth hostel.

b Kept your personal belongings tidy during the holiday.

c Helped your Patrol with the following:

- laying and clearing the tables at meal times

- preparing, cooking and serving meals

- washing, drying and putting away the crockery, cutlery and pans

- keeping the holiday home clean and tidy.

d Helped plan and lead the worship during the holiday.

2 Compile a collection of items to illustrate the various activities which you enjoyed on your holiday. This might take the form of a scrapbook or diary using photographs, postcards, maps, craft items and leaflets.

3 Explain to the tester how jobs, tasks and responsibilities were allocated to the Patrols.

4 Discuss with the tester your ideas about what to look for when choosing a place to go on a Guide Holiday, e.g. type of accommodation, possible activities, safety equipment and suitable activity wear.

5 Know what to do in case of a fire in the holiday home/youth hostel.

6 Demonstrate simple first aid for treating cuts, stings, bruises and burns.

Date:.................................

....
Tester's signature

....
My signature

HOMEMAKER

1 Do the following for seven consecutive days or four weekends (consecutive if possible).

a Clear the table and wash up after one main meal or clear the table, load and unload the dishwasher and put away the dishes.

b Air and make your bed and keep your bedroom tidy.

c Strip and make up your bed with clean bed linen (once during the time).

Take a note to the test to say that you have done everything satisfactorily.

2 Practise the following at home. The tester will ask you to do one of them at the test:

a the weekly cleaning and vacuuming of a room, and emptying the cleaner

b cleaning and disinfecting a sink, bath and toilet

c cleaning a cupboard

d defrosting and cleaning a refrigerator

e cleaning windows and washing down paintwork

f making a quick snack for the family

g laying a dinner table correctly

h cleaning a cooker

i loading and setting a washing machine.

3 Discuss with the tester how to:

a store fresh, frozen, canned and dried food

b feed a family for a week nutritiously and economically

c prevent accidents in the home

d dispose of kitchen waste.

4 Make a 'Healthy Eating Biscuit'. Give the price, weight, nutritional information, ingredients and 'best by' date of the biscuit.

Date:.............................

....
Tester's signature

....
My signature

HOME NURSE (BIENNIAL)

Note *If you hold one of the following certificates and complete Clause 6 below, you qualify for this badge: British Red Cross Society Junior Nursing Certificate, St John Ambulance Association Preliminary Certificate in Home Nursing or St Andrew's Ambulance Association Junior Certificates in Home Nursing.*

1 Know the qualities needed in a home nurse and be able to illustrate these by giving examples.

2 Know the requirements for a sick room and how to make the best use of ventilation, heating and lighting available.

3 Complete all of the following clauses:

a Show how to use and know where, in your local area, you can buy or borrow backrests, commodes and other equipment.

b Show how to make a bed with the patient in it, including the changing of sheets and arranging the pillows.

c Show the use of a drawsheet, plastic sheeting and incontinence pads.

d Show how to help a patient with the morning and evening toilet, including washing in bed, giving a mouth wash and brushing hair.

e Know which areas of the patient's body are subject to pressure in bed and how soreness of these areas can be prevented.

h

f Show how to help a patient to get up and sit in a chair. Help a patient to dress and move about the room or house.

g Take and record the temperature, pulse and respiration rate.

 4

a Know the nutritional values of food and how they help recovery from illness.

b Prepare and serve one of the following: egg custard, jelly, milk pudding, fresh fruit drink, flavoured milk drink.

c Set an invalid's tray and show how to feed and give a drink to a patient who needs help.

5

a Show how to give medicines by mouth.

b Know how to store medicines and pills safely so that they are not a danger to small children.

6 Show how to apply a cold compress, and a clean dry dressing, to any part of the arm or leg, securing it with a roller bandage.

7 Know what to include in a report for the doctor or nurse.

8 Know how infection is spread and the simple precautions to be taken when nursing an infectious patient at home.

Date:...............................

....
Tester's signature

....
My signature

HOSTESS

1 On your own, entertain the tester or someone chosen by her at a suitable event – this could be morning coffee, afternoon tea, a party or a Guide function. Lay either a table or a tray and serve her with refreshments. Be responsible for clearing away afterwards.

2 Know how to look after and entertain a guest on an overnight visit and at a party or on a brief call. You should know how to prepare a room and how to receive and introduce people.

3 Imagine you are organising a party for one of the following age groups: young children, people your own age or retired people. Make a plan for the party, an invitation and a menu. Discuss your plans for the party with the tester, explaining:

a how you will arrange the rooms

b where the guests will leave their outdoor clothes

c the toilet facilities and so on.

4 Take to the test:

a a thank-you letter with a correctly addressed envelope

b a parcel to show how you would wrap up a small present attractively.

Date:...............................

....
Tester's signature

....
My signature

INTERPRETER

Stage 1

Note *You should complete Clauses 1 and 2 and two others of your choice in one language other than your own.*

1 Famous people and places

Find out about a famous place in a country where your chosen language is spoken.

2 Using the language

At the test, in your chosen language:

a Tell the tester how you would order food and drink.

b Talk about your family.

3 Phrases

At the test, tell the tester how you would introduce yourself in your chosen language, e.g. hello, goodbye, your name.

4 Exploration

Visit or write to your nearest tourist office and find out how they could help somebody visiting the area for the first time.

5 Creation

Make a craft which is traditional from a country where your chosen language is spoken and know what it is called in that language.

Stage 2

Note *You should complete Clauses 1 and 2 and two others of your choice in one language other than your own.*

1 Famous people and places

Find out about a famous person from a country where your chosen language is spoken.

2 Using the language

At the test, in your chosen language, talk about:

a your life

b your hopes for the future.

3 Phrases

In your chosen language help the tester to get around your city or town by teaching her/him useful phrases for shopping, travel (train or bus) and sight seeing.

4 Exploration

Find out about a country where your chosen language is spoken. Tell the tester about its capital, leader, location, currency (and its relative sterling value), weather and other issues.

57

5 Creation

Learn a song from a country where your language is spoken.

Stage 3

Note *You should complete Clauses 1 and 2 and two others of your choice in one language other than your own.*

1 Famous people and places

Find out about a festival from a country where your chosen language is spoken.

2 Using the language

At the test, in your chosen language, talk about:

a   your childhood

b   your hobbies.

3 Phrases

In your chosen language help the tester to get around in your city/town by teaching her/him useful phrases when exchanging

money and traveller's cheques.

4 Exploration

Find out about places where you can get help in an emergency in a country where your chosen language is spoken, e.g. if you have lost your money, if someone needs to get home fast or if someone is ill.

5 Creation

Cook some food from a country where your chosen language is spoken, and know the names of the ingredients in that language.

Stage 4

Note *You should complete Clauses 1 and 2 and three others of your choice in one language other than your own.*

1 Famous people and places

Find out about a current issue in a country where your chosen language is spoken.

2 Using the language

At the test, in your chosen language, talk about:

a   an item of news

b   Guiding in the United Kingdom.

3 Phrases

In your chosen language describe your favourite sport or talk about a hobby.

4 Exploration

Watch a TV programme or read an article about an issue currently affecting a country where your chosen language is spoken. Talk to the tester about it and find out her/his perspective on it.

5 Creation

Cook or plan a meal where each course reflects the food eaten in a country where your chosen language is spoken.

6 Guiding

Take part in and use your language skills at an

international Guiding event.

7 Travel

Travel in a country where your chosen language is spoken. Report back to the tester.

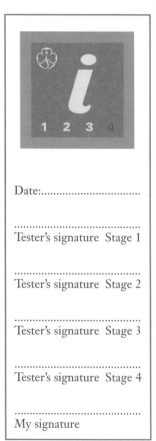

Date:...............................

....
Tester's signature Stage 1

....
Tester's signature Stage 2

....
Tester's signature Stage 3

....
Tester's signature Stage 4

....
My signature

KNITTER

Notes

- *You can start at any stage but if you start with Stages 2, 3 or 4 you must show that you can cast on and off.*

- *Knitting by hand or crochet is acceptable at any stage.*

- *Dolls' garments should not be included at any stage.*

- *Items used at one stage must not be presented again at any other stage.*

Stage 1

Notes

- *All items should be made out of school or college.*

- *If several girls are making squares, each must make at least three, and then all the squares can be sewn together to make a rug or blanket for an old person or for a charity. (See the craft publications listed in* The Guide Association Publications Catalogue *for ideas.)*

1 At the test, show the tester that you can do the following:

If you are knitting:

  a cast on and off

  b garter stitch (knit every row)

  c stocking stitch (knit and purl rows alternately).

If you crochet:

Make a loop to start, then crochet a 20cm chain and fasten off. Make at least four rows of double crochet on this chain base.

2 Use squares or diamonds – which should be at least 12cm in size – to make at least two items that can be useful either in the home or to a person, e.g. a dishcloth, mat, cushion, cot blanket, ball, purse or pot-holder. One of the items should show that you can change colours during the making.

Stage 2

Note *One item only may be made at school or college.*

1 Choose a simple pattern, and following the instructions, make a garment for a child or baby using at least two different stitches, e.g. single or double ribbing, garter, stocking or moss stitch. For crochet you may use a chain, a double or a treble chain.

2 Make another item of your choice, e.g. mittens with thumbs, a bobble hat, a scarf with tassel ends, a set of three fancy mats or a soft toy.

3 Know how to care for woollen items.

Stage 3

Note *One item only may be made at school or college and one garment may be made on a knitting machine.*

1 Following printed instructions, make a garment with sleeves, e.g. a jumper, pullover or cardigan for a child, yourself or an adult. Know how to pick up a dropped stitch.

2 Show that you understand the following terms:

If you are knitting:

  a pass the slip stitch over

  b wool forward

  c wool back

  d wool over needle

  e increase

  f decrease.

If you crochet:

  a double crochet

  b treble crochet

  c slip stitch

  d increase

  e decrease.

3 *Either*

Knit a pair of socks or gloves with fingers.

or

Crochet a garment or decorative item.

All the terms listed in Clause 2 should be demonstrated in the item made, as well as any other necessary stitches.

4 Make one other item of your choice.

5 All the items must be correctly finished and sewn up where necessary. At the test, you may be asked to demonstrate how this has been done.

6 Know how to launder and care for the items you have made. Be prepared to discuss with the tester the types of yarn used and the cost of each item.

Stage 4

Note *All items should be made out of school or college and one item may be made on a knitting machine.*

1 Make a jumper, cardigan, waistcoat, or sleeveless pullover for a child or adult using Fair Isle, Aran or another fancy pattern.

2 *Either*

Knit a small item to show the use of a cable needle.

or

Crochet a small item to illustrate the use of surface crochet or decorative edging.

3 Using leftover balls of wool, make a useful item(s) that can be given to a hospital, needy family or relief agency.

4 Discuss with the tester the different types of yarn used, their uses and costs.

Date:................................

....
Tester's signature Stage 1

....
Tester's signature Stage 2

....
Tester's signature Stage 3

....
Tester's signature Stage 4

....
My signature

KNOTTER

Hint If you can buy or borrow some of the following books you will find them useful:

Alternative Knot Book by Dr Harry Asher, published by Nautical Books

Knotting For Guides, by Hazel Bailey, published by The Guide Association

The Knot Book by Geoffrey Budworth, published by Paperfronts

Knots, Ties and Splices, revised by Commander J. Irving, published by Routledge & Kegan Paul Ltd.

Stage 1

1 Show that you can tie the following knots, bends and hitches:

  a thumb knot

  b double overhand knot

  c reef knot

  d surgeon's reef

  e reef bow

  f lark's head

  g pedigree cow hitch

  h round turn and two half hitches.

2 Choose from the knots, bends and hitches in Clause 1, and show that you can do the following:

  a Make hand loops at each end of a skipping rope.

60

b Tie a bow in shoe laces.

c Put a stopper knot at the end of a sewing thread.

d Fasten off a bandage sling.

e Put up a washing line with a different hitch at either end.

3 Make a single plait in a length of thin rope or cord.

Stage 2

Note *You should choose a suitable weight of string, cord or rope for each knot, bend or hitch.*

1 Show that you can tie the following:

a figure-of-eight knot

b packer's knot

c fisherman's knot

d sheet bend

e clove hitch

f sheepshank

g pole hitch

h slipped hitch

i halter hitch

j donkey hitch.

Explain the difference between a knot, a bend and a hitch.

2 Use the knots in Clause 1 and those in Stage 1 to do the following:

a Tie up a parcel.

b Hoist a flag.

c Shorten a guy rope or washing line that is attached to something at both ends.

d Fasten securely a bundle of poles.

e Tie up the brailing on a tent.

3 Coil a length of rope.

4 Using square lashing, West Country whipping and other appropriate knots and hitches do the following:

a Make and erect a flag pole using at least two lengths of pole.

b Make a plaited or Turk's head woggle, a net bag or a cord belt.

Stage 3

Note *You should choose a suitable weight of string, cord or rope for each knot, bend or hitch.*

1 Show that you can tie the following:

a square knot (English)

b hand knot

c chair knot

d true lover's knot

e shamrock knot

f bowline with stopper knot

g sliding figure-of-eight knot

h double fisherman's knot

i carrick bend

j figure-of-eight hitch

k marline spike hitch

l three ways of tying a clove hitch.

2 Choose from the knots in Clause 1 and those in the earlier stages to do the following:

a Make a rope ladder.

b Fasten a scarf or bow with a fancy knot.

c Tie a rope securely around another person.

d Make a handline down a slope.

3 Perform three rope tricks.

4 Using square, sheer, snake and tripod lashings make the following:

a a camp washstand

b a bridge

c a raft.

61

5 Organise a game or activity for a small group of people that involves a lot of safe knot tying.

Stage 4

1 Demonstrate the knots, bends, hitches and sinnets that you use in a sport or activity in which you are involved, e.g. rock-climbing, handicraft, boating, hairdressing, angling or service preparation. You should use the correct materials and be able to explain:

a why and when a particular knot is used

b the strengths and weaknesses of each knot

c the dangers of incorrect construction and use.

2 *Either*

With a group of people to help you, organise the building of three contrasting pioneering projects.

or

Teach a group of inexperienced knotters the knots, bends and hitches for Stage 1 or 2.

Date:.................................

....
Tester's signature Stage 1

....
Tester's signature Stage 2

....
Tester's signature Stage 3

....
Tester's signature Stage 4

....
My signature

LAUNDRESS

1 Know and understand the current International Textile Care Labelling Code.

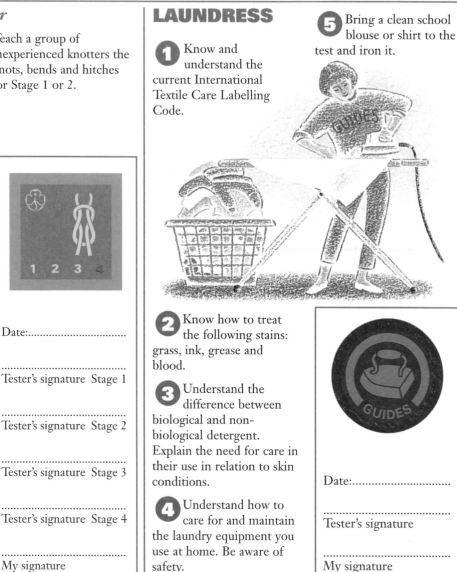

5 Bring a clean school blouse or shirt to the test and iron it.

2 Know how to treat the following stains: grass, ink, grease and blood.

3 Understand the difference between biological and non-biological detergent. Explain the need for care in their use in relation to skin conditions.

4 Understand how to care for and maintain the laundry equipment you use at home. Be aware of safety.

Date:................................

....
Tester's signature

....
My signature

LIFESAVER (BIENNIAL)

Note *Throughout this syllabus the abbreviation RLSS UK has been used for the Royal Life Saving Society of the United Kingdom and ASA for the Amateur Swimming Association.*

Stage 1

Notes

● *If you hold the RLSS UK Rookie Lifeguard 1 Star Core Award for Rescue and do Clause 5, you may have this badge.*

● *The tester can be any responsible person with relevant, up-to-date knowledge and experience.*

1 Know and understand the Water Safety Code.

2 Explain to the tester why a person making a water rescue should put her/his own safety first.

3 Explain to the tester why it is important to give clear instructions to a person whose life is in danger and how you would give a verbal rescue.

4 Demonstrate the following rescues using methods approved by the RLSS UK:

a   reaching with a rigid aid

b   reaching with an article of clothing

c   throwing a rope 3 metres

d   throwing a buoyancy aid 3 metres.

5 Explain to the tester how to summon the emergency services by telephone and when this should be done.

Stage 2

Notes

● *If you hold the RLSS UK Rookie Lifeguard Two Star Award you may have this badge.*

● *The tester should be either a teacher or examiner of lifesaving or an adult with a current RLSS UK Bronze Medallion or higher qualification.*

1 Know and understand the Water Safety Code.

2 Discuss with the tester the dangers of inland and coastal waters.

3 *Either*

Wearing a t-shirt and shorts or a skirt demonstrate the following personal survival skills:

a   A safe entry as for unknown water.

b   Tread water for two minutes.

c   Hold the HELP position for two minutes, using a lifejacket or buoyancy aid.

or

Hold ASA Personal Survival 1.

4 Demonstrate (in water) the actions of the following casualties:

a   a non-swimmer

b   a weak swimmer

c   an injured swimmer.

5 Demonstrate the following rescues using methods approved by the RLSS UK:

a   Choose appropriate aids and carry out two land-based rescues of a conscious casualty, one of which should be 2 metres from the water's edge and the other 6 metres.

b   Enter shallow water with a suitable aid and carry out a wading rescue – wade and reach or wade and throw as directed by the tester. Assist the casualty from the water.

Explain to the tester the limitations and dangers of these rescues.

6 Explain the treatment for shock and the procedure for getting medical help.

Stage 3

Notes

* *If you hold the RLSS UK Rookie Lifeguard Three Star Award you may have this badge.*

* *The tester should be a lifesaving teacher or examiner, or hold a current Award of Merit or higher qualification.*

1 Do Clauses 1, 2 and 4 of Stage 2.

2 *Either*

Wearing a long-sleeved shirt and a skirt or trousers demonstrate the following personal survival skills:

a Two safe entries. Explain to the tester when they should be used.

b Treading water for two minutes, one minute waving for help and one minute with both arms in the water.

c The HELP position. Then with at least two others, take up and hold the 'huddle' for two minutes, using lifejackets or buoyant aids.

or

Hold the ASA Personal Survival 2.

3 Demonstrate the following rescues using methods approved by the RLSS UK:

a Choose from a selection of aids and demonstrate a reaching or throwing rescue of a conscious casualty who may be anywhere between 2 and 8 metres from the edge of the water. The tester will state the type of casualty.

b Enter shallow water and demonstrate a wading rescue of a conscious casualty, using a suitable aid. The tester will state the type of casualty.

c Enter shallow water with a suitable aid and demonstrate a non-contact rescue of a casualty 20 metres away. Accompany the casualty back to safety and assist her/him to land.

d Swim 50 metres to a weak swimmer and conduct a non-contact tow for 50 metres using an aid of your choice. Assist the person to land and treat her/him for shock.

e Rescue a casualty who is unconscious and floating face down 10 metres away in deep water. Tow the casualty to shallow water and assess her/his condition. With the help of an adult, safely remove the casualty from the water. Lie the casualty on her/his back.

4 Know when and how to use expired air ventilation (EAV). Demonstrate this technique on a manikin and show the tester that you know when and how to summon qualified medical help.

5 With a person acting as the casualty, demonstrate the action you would take if a casualty vomits. Place the casualty in the recovery position.

6 Discuss with the tester how a rescuer might feel after an incident.

Stage 4

Diving to depths of greater than 1.5 metres may damage your hearing. All diving is undertaken at your own risk.

Notes

* *If you hold the RLSS UK Bronze Medallion or RLSS UK Rookie Lifeguard Four Star and do Clauses 1 and 4d, you may have this badge.*

* *Testers should have the following qualifications:*

Clause 1 – RLSS UK teacher or examiner or Guider with relevant knowledge.

Clause 2 – RLSS UK teacher or examiner or qualified swimming teacher.

Clause 3 – RLSS UK teacher or examiner.

Clause 4 – RLSS UK teacher or examiner or First Aid Instructor of recognised organisation, e.g. Red Cross, or qualified doctor/nurse.

1 Present, in an interesting way, water safety knowledge and skills to another Unit in any Section.

2 *Either*

Wearing a long-sleeved shirt or jumper and a skirt or trousers, demonstrate the following personal survival skills:

   a   Enter deep water with a straddle entry.

   b   Tread water for two minutes with one arm out of the water to wave for help (you may change arms).

   c   Swim 25 metres to a floating object.

   d   Hold the HELP position for two minutes, then with two others take up the 'huddle' position for a further two minutes.

   e   Swim 100 metres holding a floating object. Climb out from deep water without using the steps.

   f   Discuss with the tester when these skills might be used.

or

Hold ASA Personal Survival Level 2.

3 Demonstrate the following rescues using methods approved by the RLSS UK:

   a   A land-based rescue of a conscious casualty who may be anywhere between 2 and 10 metres from the edge. You may choose from a selection of aids.

   b   Swim 50 metres to a conscious casualty who is in deep water. The casualty will attempt to grab you as you approach. Show a reverse and take up the stand-off position. When it is safe to continue, conduct a non-contact tow for 50 metres finishing in deep water in the support position. Assist the casualty to land.

   c   Swim 50 metres to a conscious casualty in deep water and carry out a contact tow over 50 metres, showing good care of the casualty throughout. Finish in deep water and assist the casualty from the water. Treat her/him for shock.

   d   Swim 10 metres and recover an object or dummy from a depth of 1.5 metres, then substitute the object for a casualty and tow her/him to safety. Assess the casualty's condition and demonstrate expired air ventilation (EAV) for ten cycles whilst supporting her/him. With the help of an adult, safely remove the casualty from the water. Lie the casualty on her/his back.

4 This clause may be taken immediately after Clauses 1 to 3 or any time within the following month.

   a   Using a manikin, show how you would diagnose a cardiac arrest and demonstrate cardiopulmonary resuscitation (CPR) for at least two minutes, explaining to the tester when you would summon the emergency services.

   b   Explain the differences in adult and child EAV and CPR.

   c   With a person acting as the casualty, demonstrate the action you would take if a casualty were to vomit. Place the casualty in the recovery position.

   d   Discuss with the tester why you should summon expert help if you suspect the casualty has a spinal injury.

   e   Explain to the tester the treatment you would give to a

casualty suffering from bleeding, broken bones, asthmatic attack or hypothermia.

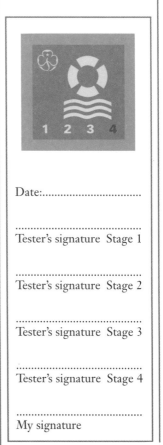

Date:...............................

....
Tester's signature Stage 1

....
Tester's signature Stage 2

....
Tester's signature Stage 3

....
Tester's signature Stage 4

....
My signature

LOCAL HISTORY

1 Find out about the origins of the city, town or village where you live. Tell the tester what you discovered.

and

Interview someone who has lived in your area for more than ten years and can tell you about the changes which have taken place during that time.

2 Do one of the following:

a Learn a local folk song and teach it to your Patrol.

b Act out a local legend with your Patrol.

c Take part in a local custom with your Patrol.

d Cook a local dish to share with your Patrol.

e Learn a local craft and share your skill with your Patrol.

f Compare the tithes

map with a present day map.

3 Make a presentation on one of the following:

a A museum, church or famous building in your area.

b The site of an archaeological dig in your area.

c A famous person connected with your area or how a well-known family has influenced your town or village.

d An industrial archaeological building or site. Find out what part it played in a local industry.

e The meaning of the Coat of Arms of your county or town.

f A building constructed of local

materials or in a local style. Find out why it was built this way.

g A subject of local historical interest that appeals to you, this might be local place names, street names, inn signs, trade signs, insurance company marks, crests or something similar.

Date:...............................

....
Tester's signature

....
My signature

MANX FOLK

1 Know:

a the words of the Manx National Anthem

b the composition of the Manx flag

c the motto and its meaning.

2 Make a scrapbook or some visual record to illustrate interesting features of the Isle of Man, its scenery, the main occupations of the people and its traditions.

3 Do any two of the following:

a Tell a Manx folk story.

b Sing a Manx song.

c Take part in a Manx folk dance.

4 Show an understanding of the current position of the Isle of Man in relation to:

a the United Kingdom

b the European Union.

5 Know the date of Tynwald day and be able to describe simply what happens on that occasion.

6

a Dress a doll in Manx costume.

b Cook something typically Manx.

Date:.............................

....
Tester's signature

....
My signature

MAPREADER

1 Find a place on a map by grid reference, and find the grid reference of a given place (you should use the six-figure grid references).

and

Know what scale, for distance and contours, means on a map. On a map, measure the distance between two places and the difference in height between two points.

2 Set a map:

a with a compass

b without a compass, for example by using the sun, stars and landmarks.

3 Be able to find the way from one point to another following a street map and an Ordnance Survey 1:50,000 or 1:25,000 map.

One of these will be selected by your tester for a practical demonstration out of doors. This may be on foot, on a bicycle, on horseback or in a vehicle.

4 Using the necessary conventional mapping signs, make a rough map from a description given by your tester.

and

From an Ordnance Survey 1:50,000 or 1:25,000 map write a description of a 4.8 to 8 km (3 to 5 miles) walk chosen by your tester.

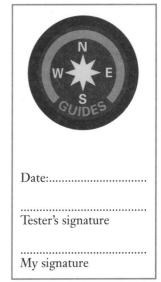

Date:.............................

....
Tester's signature

....
My signature

MUSICIAN

Stage 1

1 Play or sing two contrasting pieces.

2 Sing one verse of the National Anthem.

3 Show the tester you can read music by being able to name the lines and spaces in the treble clef, and by clapping a simple rhythm.

4 Make a percussion instrument and, using it, compose a simple percussion accompaniment to a well-known song.

Stage 2

1 Sing two verses of the National Anthem.

2 Play two contrasting pieces.

3 Make a scrapbook about some aspect of music you really enjoy. Be prepared to discuss this book with the tester. You may also wish to include tapes and/or records.

4 Sing or play at sight simple music provided by the tester.

5 Show that you have used your musical skills for the enjoyment of others.

6 Sustain a second part – either alto or descant – to a tune of your own choice while the tester plays the melody.

Stage 3

1 Prepare a 15-minute musical programme to perform to the tester.

2 Take to the test a composition of about 16 bars in length written by yourself. Be prepared to perform it.

3 Discuss with the tester your playing (or singing) and composition.

Consider your choice of repertoire and answer questions on style and expression.

4 Show that you continue to use your musical skills for the enjoyment of others on a regular basis.

5 Discuss with the tester some aspect of music which interests you. Illustrate your discussion with tapes, CDs or records.

Date:................................

....
Tester's signature Stage 1

....
Tester's signature Stage 2

....
Tester's signature Stage 3

....
My signature

MUSIC LOVER

1 Tell the tester about the music you enjoy. You could talk to her about the composers, writers, performers and instrumentalists.

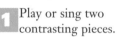

2 Keep a diary of concerts, shows, gigs and other performances you have heard or been to. The performances could have been live or may be television or radio broadcasts.

3 Put together a presentation for your Patrol demonstrating the sort of music that you enjoy. You should include posters, programmes, photographs and so on in your presentation, as well as examples of the music.

Date:..............................

....
Tester's signature

....
My signature

NEEDLECRAFT

Notes

• *At Stages 2, 3 and 4, it is assumed that you can thread a needle, and start and finish off the work yourself.*

• *Items made for one stage must not be presented again at another stage.*

• *Commercial paper patterns are expensive so borrowing and sharing is encouraged (which means that they must be used carefully). Magazines often offer free patterns.*

Stage 1

Notes

• *Only one item may be made at school or college.*

• *The type of fabric used will vary according to your age, e.g. Binca, evenweave, plain cotton. Use needle and thread suitable for the material, e.g. tapestry wool, wool, embroidery silk, etc.*

1 Show that you can thread a needle, and start and finish off your work.

2 Make two of the following items:

a a bookmark

b a purse

c a pencil case

d a book cover (e.g. for your Handbook)

e a beach bag

f a place mat

or something similar and decorate both using at least four of the following stitches: chain, stem, blanket, cross, fly, satin, threaded running stitch or whipped running stitch.

Stage 2

Note *Only one item may be made at school or college.*

1 Show you can tack and hem by sewing a badge onto your uniform or a name tape onto a garment by hand.

2 Use a simple pattern to make a useful article of your choice. You may use a sewing machine. Tell the tester how the pattern was placed on the material.

3 Sew a button by hand onto a garment. Know how to sew on two-hole and four-hole buttons, and those with a shank.

4 Make an item of your choice using a different form of needlecraft, e.g. tapestry, appliqué (by hand or machine), embroidery, etc. You may not use knitting or crochet.

Stage 3

Notes

• *Only one item may be made at school or college.*

• *Your work should show that you can sew by hand and use a sewing machine.*

1 Have a working knowledge of a sewing machine.

2 Make a simple garment for yourself, and be able to say how you laid the pattern on the fabric, and how you made up the garment.

3 Discuss with the tester the importance of the different types, sizes and uses of needles – especially those used at this stage.

4 Make an item for a bedroom, e.g. a wall hanging, a cushion cover, a soft toy, a laundry bag, a holdall, or a picture, using one of the following methods:

a patchwork

b tapestry

c appliqué (by hand or machine)

d soft sculpture

e embroidery (machine, traditional, Hardanger, cross-stitch, etc.)

f bargello.

5 Know what is meant by the International Textile Care Labelling Code, and how you would care for the items you have made. Understand the importance of labels in bought items.

Stage 4

Notes

● *Only one item may be made at school or college.*

● *Your work should show a good standard of hand and machine sewing.*

1 Know the following:

a the difference between natural and man-made fibres, and how to care for and launder each type

b the suitability of fabrics for different types of garment

c the importance of using the right thread and trimmings for each fabric.

2 Make a garment, using fabric of your choice, from a paper pattern. It should include at least four of the following processes:

a two methods of making seams

b neatening raw edges

c disposing of fulness

d finishing a hem

e setting in a sleeve

f making a buttonhole

g setting on a collar

h putting in a zip

i putting in a pocket or applying a patch pocket.

Discuss with the tester the costing and method of making up the garment.

3 Learn a form of needlecraft that you have not used before either in this badge or in any other Interest Badge. Use it to make a useful item for personal or home use.

Date:...............................

....
Tester's signature Stage 1

....
Tester's signature Stage 2

....
Tester's signature Stage 3

....
Tester's signature Stage 4

....
My signature

OARSWOMAN

Stage 1

Note *The tester should be aged 16 or over and hold The Guide Association Oarsman Permit or have an equivalent knowledge and be acceptable to the County Assistant Outdoor Activities Adviser (Boating).*

1 Swim 50 metres and stay afloat for five minutes wearing clothes. This may be done in a swimming pool and you may wear a buoyancy aid if you wish.

2 Wear suitable clothing and a buoyancy aid (unless using unclassified water) for the test and be able to explain their importance to the tester.

3 Name the parts of a boat.

4 Demonstrate either by yourself or as one of a crew:

a preparing the boat and launching

b leaving shore or jetty

c rowing a course including turning, backing and stopping

d coming alongside a jetty or coming ashore

e putting away boat and equipment.

5 Demonstrate how to use either a round turn and two half hitches or a bowline for tying up a boat.

6 Understand boat discipline and how to behave towards other water users. Know the rules for meeting, passing and crossing other craft and any local rules about access and use of the water.

7 Point out any hazards on the water you are using. Know how to call for assistance.

Stage 2

Note *If you complete The Guide Association Oarsman Permit, you may have this badge. The syllabus is in* Qualifications, *published by The Guide Association.*

Stage 3

Note *If you complete the syllabus of the Guide Association Rowing Charge Permit you may have this badge. The syllabus is in* Qualifications.

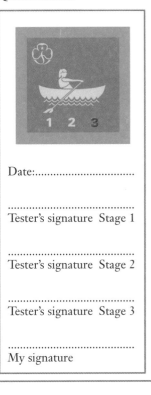

Date:.................................

....
Tester's signature Stage 1

....
Tester's signature Stage 2

....
Tester's signature Stage 3

....
My signature

OBSERVER

Remember to tell an adult before you go out alone.

Part I General Observation

Pass two of the following clauses to be chosen by your tester:

1 Follow a route for 0.8km (0.5 miles) by means of a trail or sketch map and answer correctly questions based on the route covered (for example 15 out of 20).

2 After five minutes' observation describe a person's appearance and manner.

3 Spend 15 minutes in the open and make a list of sounds heard or listen to a tape recording and identify sounds.

4 Identify nine out of 12 substances by smell.

5 Identify 15 out of 20 objects by touch.

Part II Project

Pass one of the following clauses chosen in consultation with your tester:

6 Make a sketch map of an area showing the position of trees and shrubs.

7 Make a survey of the plant life of an area.

8 Keep a daily record of the weather for a week, including notes on temperature, amount and type of cloud, sunshine and precipitation.

9 Watch a chosen area for a week and report on its bird and/or animal and/or insect life.

10 Take at least 12 photographs to illustrate distinctive features of trees, plants, wild animals, etc.

Part III
Identification

Pass two of the following clauses. Consult the tester before making your choice.

11 Recognise 12 trees. Describe their leaves, winter twigs, flowers and fruits. Know their use to campers and hikers.

12 Recognise 20 plants.

13 Recognise ten birds by appearance, flight, call or song.

14 Recognise eight constellations or stars.

15 Recognise ten sea-shore specimens (shells, seaweeds etc.)

16 Recognise ten different butterflies, moths and/or other insects.

17 Recognise ten different aircraft, ships or cars.

Your tester may appoint another responsible person to test this section.

Date:.............................

....
Tester's signature

....
My signature

OUTDOOR CHEF

1 Bring to the test evidence (such as a letter from an adult or other badges you have gained) of previous cooking out of doors in two of the following ways:

a on a camp altar fire

b on a hike fire without utensils

c on a barbecue

d on a portable stove

e in a camp oven, on a sawdust boiler or in a haybox.

A record should be shown of the dishes cooked. One of the other methods on the list should be demonstrated at the test.

2 At the test, prepare, cook, serve attractively and clear away:

a a starter or an appetiser

b a main course

c a pudding or sweet

d coffee, tea or cocoa.

The recipes for the starter or appetiser, the main course and the pudding or sweet should be handed to the tester beforehand. All food should be prepared at the test. The ingredients should be stored correctly while in transit and awaiting cooking. There should be a nutritious balance of fresh and convenience food. Taste and appearance are important. The candidate and tester should eat together. Safety, hygiene, clearing up and disposal of rubbish should be of a high standard. You must provide all the necessary equipment.

Date:.............................

....
Tester's signature

....
My signature

OUTDOOR COOK

Notes

● *You may take a Guide friend with you to help you. If your friend wishes to be tested for this badge at the same time both of you must share the preparation and work for the test and be able to satisfy the tester that your efforts were equal.*

● *The tester should be an experienced camper.*

Cooking for the test should ideally be done on an open-wood fire, but if you cannot find a site where wood fires are permitted, you may use a portable stove instead.

1

a   Collect and stack suitable firewood. Know the precautions to take when lighting fires and cooking out of doors.

b   If you are cooking on a portable stove, know the safety precautions for using your stove. Explain to the tester

how to refuel your stove. Demonstrate if possible.

2 Cook an appetising, balanced meal for two people out of doors on a wood fire. There should be at least two cooked courses and a hot drink. At least three cooking methods should be used and one dish should be nutritious and should include one fresh vegetable or fruit and one other fresh food.

3 Show the tester how you have packed your food to bring it to the test and that you have stored it correctly before it is cooked.

4 Prepare all food at the test. Demonstrate how to keep food hot. Clear away and wash up after the meal. Dispose of all rubbish and clear up the fire correctly.

5 Make up and be able to use a pocket first-aid kit suitable for coping with accidents which may arise when cooking out of doors. Know how to treat burns and scalds.

Date:.............................

....
Tester's signature

....
My signature

73

OUTDOOR PURSUITS

O/p

1 Undertake at least two sessions in any three of the following: abseiling, archery, canoeing, dry slope skiing, orienteering, pioneering, rafting, rock climbing, sailing, boardsailing, rowing, wayfaring, skiing or similar activities. Be prepared to talk about them to the tester and if possible bring photos of the event.

2 Discuss with the tester the clothing and equipment needed for your chosen activities.

3 Know the safety rules for your chosen activities.

The activities do not all have to be taken at the same event – they could be done over a series of events.

Date:..............................

....
Tester's signature

....
My signature

PATHFINDER

Note *All places are to be chosen by the tester.*

1 Know your neighbourhood thoroughly. Be able to give clear directions on the easiest and quickest way to get to places within a 0.8km (0.5 mile) radius if you live in a town, or a 1.6km (1 mile) radius if you live in the country, of your home or Guide headquarters.

You should be able to give directions to the following types of places e.g. police station, bus and railway station, place of worship, toilets, telephone, post office, post box, places of interest.

At the test, draw a sketch map showing the way from one given point to another.

2 Give directions to any place chosen by the tester within an 8km (5 mile) radius in country areas or 3km (2 mile) radius in urban areas using available public transport and knowing main destinations.

3 Know the opening hours of local shops, garages, petrol stations, post office and library.

4 Be able to find north by the sun, stars and a compass.

5 Find the way from one given place to

another by use of both a street map and a motorist's road map (for example a map with a scale of 1 inch:3 miles).

Show the tester on one of the maps the route you would take between two places given by the tester. Using the other type of map demonstrate practically, out of doors, how you would get to two places given by the tester.

In an area where no street map is available an Ordnance Survey map may be used.

Date:..............................

....
Tester's signature

....
My signature

PHOTOGRAPHER

Stage 1

1 Tell the tester about your camera and how you use it to take good pictures. You should know the following:

a what size film it takes

b how to load and unload the film

c how to keep your camera clean and remove dust and grit safely.

2 Take 12 prints or transparencies either at a Guide Association event or holiday, or on a chosen theme e.g. animals or landscape. The set of prints must include the following:

a landscapes

b people

c action shots.

The prints should be mounted (as a display or in an album) or presented to show the chosen event or theme clearly to the members of your Six, Patrol or Unit.

Stage 2

Note: *When you have been using your camera for six months do Clauses 1, 2 and 3 and choose one from Clauses 4, 5 or 6.*

1 Know how your camera works, and be able to explain to the tester its special functions (e.g. automatic focus and automatic wind), and how they can help your photography.

2 Know the functions of the different parts of the camera such as the lens, shutter and stops. Explain briefly how a negative and a positive of a print or transparency are produced.

3 Be able to tell the tester any or all of the following:

a how a lens hood can improve photographs

b the purpose of an ultra violet or skylight filter

c what camera shake is, and how to avoid it

d how to achieve the best angles and lighting to show your subject to the best advantage

e how to avoid 'red eye' when using a flash.

4 Bring to the test a collection of 20 prints taken over a period of six months. They should be mounted as for an exhibition with captions, as far as possible. The collection should include the following:

a a sequence of five photographs (which may have been taken at different times) either telling a story or showing different aspects of the subject

b other prints which show at least two of the following subjects: landscape, nature, portrait, architecture, action, backlighting.

Be able to talk about your pictures to your Six, Patrol or Unit.

5

a Make a collection of at least 20 slides, covering two of the subjects given in Clause 4b.

b *either*

Give a slide show to your Six, Patrol or Unit.

or

Have the slides made into prints and exhibit them with captions, as described in Clause 4.

6 For the test (which can be taken in your home or anywhere with suitable equipment), show a five-minute video film you have made, which demonstrates your understanding of the different techniques required to produce an enjoyable programme. The film may be about:

  a   a Guiding event or family holiday

  b   a story with commentary or sound effects (which need not be on the film).

If possible, show the video film to your Six, Patrol or Unit.

Stage 3

Note *When you have been using your camera for at least 12 months, mount an exhibition of photographs or slides, or give a video presentation. Choose and complete Clause 1, 2 or 3.*

1 Black and White and Colour Negative Photography

  a   Mount an exhibition of at least ten prints of either different aspects of a single happening or a series of happenings at Guiding events or at a club to which you belong.

  b   The photographs must be at least 5 x 7 inches (12.7 x 17.8cm), and they should have suitable captions for display to the public. At least half should show some action. All the photographs must have been taken by you and, where possible, developed and printed by you.

  c   The photographs should illustrate the following subjects: still life, portrait, group, landscape, nature, action.

  d   Use the appropriate techniques from the following: contre jour, table top, fill-in-flash, available light. Discuss your choice with the tester and be prepared to show that you understand the meaning of the techniques you did not use.

2 Colour Transparencies (Slides)

  a   Mount an exhibition of slides suitable for a public meeting (e.g. an Annual General Meeting). All the transparencies should have been taken by you, and there should be either a live commentary or a properly recorded and synchronised commentary with suitable music. The requirements are the same as for Clause 1.

  b   You will be asked to:

  • demonstrate how to mount slides

  • explain the advantages and disadvantages of card and glass mounts

  • describe the care of both types of mount

  • explain the importance of storage of slides, and the results of bad storage.

3 Video Photography

  a   You will be asked to do the following:

  • Describe the features you would

look for when buying a video camera and why you would need them.

- Explain how to care for your camera and which parts should be regularly cleaned, how they should be cleaned and which parts should not be touched.

- Explain the markings on your camera, e.g. F numbers, m, ft, fps, etc. and know how to use them to get the effects you want.

- Know what 'depth of field' means and how to use it.

- Know what LED stands for, what all the LEDs indicate, and what action to take (also on any other equipment you may be using, e.g. VCR or projector).

- Explain the essential differences

between video and still photography, the cameras used for each, the difficulties a video photographer is likely to face, and the techniques of a good video.

b Make a video with sound lasting eight to ten minutes. All shooting, editing and production should be by you. Choose one of the following themes:

- a documentary on Guiding for public showing

- a record of an event or series of events in your District, Division or County suitable for showing at an Annual General Meeting

- a recruiting film for the Senior Section suitable for showing to Brownies or Guides

- a publicity film about Rangers or Young Leaders

suitable for showing to other interested organisations or to the public.

The film must demonstrate at least three of the following techniques: zooming, tilt shot, macro, voice-over, panning to cover landscape. All techniques should be discussed with the tester.

c Understand the significance of the figures and developing instructions on the film carton and on the cassette or wrapper (e.g. ISO Din, C41). Know how to load and unload a 35mm and a roll film camera, and what precautions to take.

d Explain the effects of the following:

- lens hood and filters – black and white as well as colour

- skylight or ultra violet filters over the lens (in greater

depth than explained in Stage 2).

e Describe any new ways you may have found of counteracting or minimising camera shake.

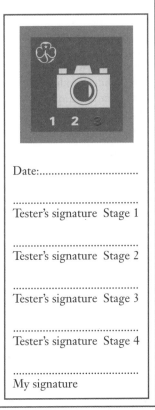

Date:...............................

....
Tester's signature Stage 1

....
Tester's signature Stage 2

....
Tester's signature Stage 3

....
Tester's signature Stage 4

....
My signature

RADIO COMMUNICATION

Note *A Guide who holds an Amateur Radio Licence, an Amateur Radio Certificate or is a holder of the Amateur Novice Licence may have this badge.*

1 Keep a log of at least 20 different amateur radio stations heard within a two-month period. If you have suitable equipment at least five stations should be outside the United Kingdom. The log should include the date, time, callsign, frequency and, when known, the location of each station.

2 Complete all the following sections:

a Know the internationally recommended phonetic alphabet. Spell aloud phonetically simple words including your first name and home town. Interpret words which the tester spells aloud phonetically.

b Know the country prefixes for the callsigns of ten countries and the call sign prefixes for the different areas of the United Kingdom.

c Know the meaning of five international Q-codes. Explain the reason for their use.

3

a Discuss with the tester the basic sections of a radio system.

b Explain how radio waves are propagated over long and short distances.

c Discuss with the tester safety at an amateur radio station.

4 Do two of the following:

a Help with a Thinking Day on the Air or other special event station.

b Prepare and read aloud a greeting message to last not more than two minutes.

c Design a QSL (confirmation of contact) card for a Guide station. Show how to fill in the details of a contact.

d Construct a simple receiver for any radio frequency and tell the tester how it works. Published circuits or kits may be used.

e Show how to tune a radio receiver on more than one frequency band to give the best reception.

f Arrange for your Patrol to visit an amateur radio station. Be able to talk to your Patrol about the station.

g Be able to recognise by sound individual Morse code letters and numbers.

Date:.............................

....
Tester's signature

....
My signature

READER

1 Show the tester how you would go about finding a book in your local or school library, using the catalogue.

2 Know what is meant by the following words: author, title, publisher, non-fiction and reference book.

3 Tell the tester about six books you have read recently. They should be written by different authors and one must be an information book.

4 Do one of the following:

a Find out about reading facilities for people with disabilities e.g. large print books, talking newspapers, Braille books, reading machines.

b Write a book review and discuss it with the tester.

c Make a bookmark and tell the tester about the care and repair of books.

5 Know how to use a contents page and index of a book, and how to find something in an encyclopaedia.

Date: 3/8/95

Tester's signature

My signature

RIDER

A rider with a disability should take the test where she is known.

Stage 1

Note *If you hold the Pony Club D Test Certificate or the Riding for the Disabled Association Proficiency Test Grade 3 Award, you may have this badge.*

1 Show the tester that you know how to dress appropriately and understand the importance of wearing a hard hat.

2 Demonstrate or explain how to:

a approach a pony or horse correctly using aids if necessary

b catch a pony or horse and put on a head-collar/halter

c lead a pony or horse in hand

d give a pony or horse an apple or carrot.

3 Be able to:

a mount and dismount correctly

b demonstrate the correct position in the saddle and hold the reins correctly

c ride a quiet pony or horse in an enclosed area without a leading rein and stop, walk, turn and trot safely.

4 Know how to ride along and across a road with an adult accompanying you.

r

79

5 Know the basic needs of a grass-kept pony or horse in summer and winter, e.g. feeding, watering and grooming.

6 Identify:

a the simple points of a pony or horse

b some parts of a saddle and bridle.

Stage 2

Note *If you hold the Pony Club D Plus Certificate or the Riding for the Disabled Association Proficiency Test Grade 4 Award, you may have this badge.*

1 Demonstrate or explain how to control a quiet pony or horse on the road or in the countryside. You should be able to:

a use simple leg and hand aids effectively

b make simple turns and circles in walk and trot

c canter over a single pole and a very small fence

d walk without stirrups

e alter your stirrups and tighten or loosen your girth while mounted.

2 Show that you understand the Green Cross Code as it applies to riders and the importance of thanking considerate drivers and pedestrians.

3 Know something about caring for your pony or horse. Demonstrate or explain how to:

a put on a saddle and bridle (with a snaffle bit)

b clean a saddle and bridle

c lead a pony or horse in hand at walk and trot

d tie up a pony or horse correctly

e pick up and pick out feet.

4 Identify the essential items of a grooming kit and know how they are used.

5 Know the common colours and markings of a pony or horse.

Stage 3

Note *If you hold the Pony Club C Test Certificate and complete Clause 11 or hold the Riding for the Disabled Association Proficiency Test Grade 6 Award, you may have this badge.*

1 Present yourself and your pony well.

Riding

2 Show that you can control your mount, have a seat independent of the reins and can maintain the correct position of your hands at walk, trot and canter. You should be able to do the following:

a Use the correct aids to increase and decrease pace; turn circles at walk, trot and canter; canter on a named leg on a circle.

b Ride up and down hills and jump low fences in good style.

c Trot without stirrups.

3 Understand the care needed when riding in the countryside and across farmland.

Road Safety

4 Know the Highway Code as it applies to riders and demonstrate an awareness of possible dangers while riding on the roads.

Stable Management

5 Know how to clean and care for saddlery.

6 Know the main points of feeding and watering ponies or horses and understand the importance of cleanliness.

7 Show that you know how to saddle, bridle and rug up a pony or horse.

8 Understand the care and working of a grass-kept pony or horse.

9 Know when a pony or horse needs shoeing and recognise when it is lame.

10 Know the main indicators for health in a pony or horse and how to treat minor wounds.

Progress

11 Keep a record of your stable management and riding activities for three months, noting any improvements.

Stage 4

Note *If you hold the Pony Club C Plus Test Certificate and complete Clause 9 or hold the Riding for the Disabled Association Proficiency Test Grade 7 Award, you may have this badge.*

Riding

1 Show that you are a competent rider with a secure seat independent of the reins and understand the correct application of the aids. You should be able to do the following:

a Sitting trot; rising trot on either diagonal; change the diagonal.

b Ride up and down steep hills and jump fences and ditches at trot and canter.

c Change leg at canter through trot.

d Open a simple gate without dismounting.

e Canter without stirrups.

Road Safety

2 Show that you understand the Highway Code as it applies to riders and know how to behave when riding in company.

Stable Management

3 Know how to care for and work both a pony or horse off-grass and a stabled pony or horse. Understand why and how feeding, watering regimes and work have to be varied according to whether the pony or horse is stabled or grass-kept.

4 Know the structure of a pony's or horse's foot. Watch a farrier at work and know the names of the farrier's essential tools.

5 Demonstrate or explain how to fit a saddle and bridle and understand the importance of well-fitting tack.

6 Recognise and know how to put on a rug, tail bandage, travel bandages and a roller.

7 Know when a pony or horse is lame or in poor condition and be able to recognise minor ailments.

8 Have an understanding of basic first aid and be able to carry out basic treatment for wounds, ailments and lameness prescribed by a vet.

9 Do one of the following and be prepared to talk to the tester about what you have learned:

a Choose an equestrian sport e.g. show jumping, eventing or dressage. Read a book about it and find out about a sporting personality involved in the sport.

b Build up a scrapbook or file of information on the equestrian subject of your choosing.

Date:...............................

....
Tester's signature Stage 1

....
Tester's signature Stage 2

....
Tester's signature Stage 3

....
Tester's signature Stage 4

....
My signature

ROAD SAFETY

1 Tell the tester what are the main causes of road accidents to children of your own age in your area.

2 Design a poster or leaflet for a special road-safety campaign, for example being seen by night and day.

3 Show in your own way that you understand the road-safety problems for:

a children younger than yourself

b your Patrol

c elderly people

d disabled people

e animals.

4 Know the Highway Code as it applies to pedestrians and cyclists together with an understanding of traffic lights, signs, road markings and signals given by road users and police.

5 Know how to summon help in the event of a road accident.

Date:...............................

....
Tester's signature

....
My signature

82

SCIENCE INVESTIGATOR

You should make sure that you carry out all your investigations with care to safety.

Hint The Guide Association publish a pack of activity cards called *Science and Technology Fun* with lots of ideas for activities. Ask your Guider if she has a copy or find out if your Patrol or unit can buy one. It is available from Guide Association Trading Service, Guide shops and depots.

Keep a record of all your investigations and be prepared to tell the tester about them. You may have to talk about projects with different testers.

1 Carry out all the investigations in this clause:

a Wire a plug and find out about the correct fuses required for different appliances.

b Find out how the gears on a bicycle work and explain their action.

c Tell the tester about five sources of energy used in this country.

d Design and make a device to measure lung capacity.

2 Choose and carry out three projects from the following:

a Write a report on the energy efficiency of the building where you meet for Guides and suggest any possible improvements.

b Make a fire extinguisher from household items and use it outside.

c Design and make an instrument for measuring distance.

d Build a personal alarm that could be easily activated from your pocket.

e Build a machine to transport a large object (e.g. an empty Patrol box or suitcase) over a distance of 10 metres.

f Make a device to project a ping-pong ball at least 2 metres into a bucket. Demonstrate the accuracy of your device four out of five times, using a piece of A4 card, two rubber bands and sticky tape.

3 Choose one technical advancement which has been made in your lifetime and tell the tester about it.

Date:...............................

....
Tester's signature

....
My signature

SCOTTISH FOLK

Hint Information is available from The Guide Association (Scotland) at 16 Coates Crescent, Edinburgh, EH3 7AH.

1 Know the composition of the Scottish flag and tell the story of St Andrew.

2 Make an interesting presentation such as a display, talk, scrapbook, with commentary on one of the following:

a a visit to a place of interest e.g. a Scottish museum, country house, folk museum, castle or battlefield

b some of the crafts, folklore and traditions of your area.

3 Do one of the following:

a Play a traditional Scottish tune on an instrument of your choice.

b Sing a traditional song – from your own area.

c Perform a Scottish dance that is new to you, such as Scottish country dancing or Highland.

d Recite a poem in Gaelic, Scottish or other local dialect. Discuss it with your tester.

e Tell a story derived from Scottish folklore or history.

4 Give the meaning of ten Scottish or Gaelic place names.

5 Do one of the following:

a Using a recipe, prepare, make and serve a traditional Scottish dish, such as oatcakes, shortbread, Scotch broth.

b Knit something incorporating a traditional Scottish pattern, such as Shetland, Eriskay, Fair Isle.

c Collect some sheep's wool. Cord, spin and dye it using natural materials. (In the interest of conservation lichens must not be used.)

d Make an article with a Celtic or Pictish design; you may use materials/threads of your own choice.

Date:...............................

....
Tester's signature

....
My signature

SEASONS

Note *If you gained the Seasons Badge as a Brownie, you need only do Clauses 1, 2, 3 and one from Clause 4, which you should add to the record you kept as a Brownie.*

1 Know the position of the earth in relation to the sun in each of the four seasons and explain the characteristics of each season.

2 Explain the meaning of the terms 'solstice' and 'equinox'.

3 Make a collection of poems, stories or music which suggests the four seasons to you. Your collection should include at least two from each season. Discuss your choice with your tester.

4 Choose three from the following and do them in the appropriate season:

a With the help of your Patrol demonstrate to the tester four British folk customs, one from each season.

b Collect some blackberries, tomatoes or apples and make a pie, jam or chutney.

c Make a traditional British meal suitable to the season in which you take this badge.

d Make a bird table and nest box and with permission fix them in a suitable position. Keep a record of any activity around them for at least a month.

e Be able to recognise the different cloud formations and the weather associated with them.

f Grow some bulbs or a pot plant from seed or cutting.

Date:.............................

....
Tester's signature

....
My signature

SECRETARY

1 Keep one of the following:

a a record of your Patrol's activities or personal record or diary for two consecutive months

b a detailed logbook of a week's Guide camp or holiday

c a record of decisions taken and accurate minutes of a meeting which you regularly attend such as Patrol Leaders' Council or Patrol in Council.

2 Keep the accounts for either personal funds or your secretarial expenses for two consecutive months.

Show that you know the need to budget either weekly or monthly.

3 Know how to write a cheque, and how to make payments by post. Find out what postal services are available, including recorded delivery and registered post.

4 Show that you can do the following and be prepared to write one at the test:

a a letter inviting neighbouring Guides to spend an afternoon or evening with your Unit, stating time, place, details of the event, number of Guides etc.

b a letter accepting such an invitation

c a letter of apology explaining your absence from a Guide event

d a letter of thanks for a gift received, either personally or on behalf of the Patrol

e a letter ordering goods by mail order and enclosing payment, or a request for further information from an advertisement

f an application for a job or CV.

5 Write a report of 200 to 300 words suitable for a magazine or newspaper about a Guide event you have attended, or a newsletter for your Unit or Patrol.

Date:.............................

....
Tester's signature

....
My signature

S SIGHT AWARENESS

Hint The Royal National Institute for the Blind (RNIB) Head Office is at: 224 Great Portland Street, London W1N 6AA. Look in the telephone directory for the address and telephone number of your local organisation.

Stage 1

1 Make a collage or sculpture which a blind or partially sighted person can handle and describe. Try to use materials which will feel interesting.

2 Find out and tell your tester about Guide Dogs for the Blind and how they are trained.

3 Identify six objects correctly by touch and six by smell.

4 Explain how to approach and introduce yourself to a blind or partially sighted person.

Stage 2

1 Make a short recording of at least three stories or articles you would like to share with a blind person of your own age.

2 Know something of the work of one of the National Voluntary Organisations who serve the needs of blind or partially sighted people such as:

- Royal National Institute for the Blind
- British Talking Book Service
- Sense

Share this information with members of your Unit.

3 Take part in a game or activity in your Unit wearing either a blindfold or a pair of covered glasses.

4 Tell the tester about the different coloured canes, their use and meaning, and find your way around a room blindfolded but with the aid of a cane.

Stage 3

1 Using an alphabet card if necessary, read a message in Grade 1 Braille and write in your Promise using a Braille Frame and Stylus so that a third person may read it.

2 Find out something about a famous blind person, e.g. Louis Braille, Helen Keller, Laura Bridgeman, Arthur Sculthorpe or David Blunkett MP, and tell the tester what you have learned.

3 Find out about local organisations/facilities for the blind e.g. talking newspapers, sports associations, scented gardens.

4 List three hazards that people may encounter because of sight loss and what safety devices are available, e.g. around pedestrian crossings, cooker knobs and liquid level indicators.

5 Know the best way to guide a blind person. Lead a blindfolded partner and guide that person to a chair.

6 Describe the shape and contents of a room so that a blind or blindfolded person can safely negotiate her or his way around it.

Stage 4

1 Learn the deaf blind alphabet and use it to introduce yourself. Teach the deaf blind alphabet to a group and design some activities to practise its use.

2 Find out about the history of aids for improving vision, e.g. glasses, contact lenses, and the causes and treatment of blindness.

3 Find out what it is like to be blind or partially sighted by talking to someone with this disability. Find out how they overcome some of the difficulties they encounter and explain this to the tester.

4 Experience for yourself what it is like to be led by someone using

the 'Sighted Guide' technique while your vision is artificially impaired.

5 Make or adapt a game for a child with a vision impairment.

6 *Either*

Design something which will enable a blind person to become more independent.

or

Learn 'Sighted Guide' skills and (for approximately ten minutes) be able to guide the tester safely round a route chosen together using appropriate strategies to overcome any problems.

The route should include:

a crossing a road

b steps or stairs

c a doorway

d reaching for an object.

Date:................................

....
Tester's signature Stage 1

....
Tester's signature Stage 2

....
Tester's signature Stage 3

....
Tester's signature Stage 4

....
My signature

SINGER

1 Sing four songs, each from a different land. At least one song must be in a foreign language.

2 Improvise a second part to a well-known song chosen by the tester. (She will let you have the words and tune before the day of the test.)

3 *Either*

Sing an original song, the words and music of which you have written yourself.

or

Write new words to an existing tune.

4 Teach three suitable action songs to one of the following:

a your Patrol

b local Brownie Pack

c local Rainbow Unit.

5 Take your own collection of the words and music of 20 or more songs to the test. These songs must not be photocopied from books. Ask your Guider about

copyright. Know where the material comes from, such as song books or tapes and records currently published by The Guide Association. This could be the start of your own campfire song book.

Date:................................

....
Tester's signature

....
My signature

S SPEAKER

Note *In group work at all stages, you should show that you are able to listen, and respond in a relevant way, to other people. Speech should be audible, and, if a microphone is necessary, you should know how to use it correctly.*

Stage 1

1 Tell the tester about one of your hobbies or about an interesting experience you have had.

2 Take part in a group discussion, e.g. to plan something.

3 Recite or read aloud a poem or short prose passage of your choice.

4 Thank someone for something they have done for you or given to you.

5 Ask permission for something.

6 Listen to a verbal message, and then repeat it to someone.

Stage 2

1 Give a prepared informal talk (using notes if you want) to a group about a hobby or interesting experience.

2 Take part in a group discussion, e.g. to plan something, then report the arguments and conclusion to someone.

3 *Either*

Read aloud a passage of your choice from the writings of your faith.

or

Lead prayers.

4 Introduce two people to each other, using normal conventions.

5 Know how to introduce a guest speaker.

6 Give clear explanation or directions, e.g. of how to do something or how to get somewhere.

Stage 3

1 Give a prepared informal talk (using notes if you want) on a topic that interests you. The talk should show a clear structure. You should be prepared to answer questions on it afterwards, and to describe how you would use visual aids, including an overhead projector, to illustrate your talk.

2 Take part in one of the following activities, or something similar:

a   a radio game, e.g. 'Just a Minute'

b   a hat debate

c   a balloon debate.

3 Read aloud a passage of your choice that was written for a particular purpose, such as to persuade or to amuse.

4 Chair an informal discussion.

5 Be able to give a vote of thanks.

6 Explain the techniques of speaking to less experienced speakers, e.g.

the need to vary intonation, and the use of pauses, pitch, stress, pace, gesture and eye contact. Where possible, demonstrate how it should be done.

Stage 4

1 Give a prepared formal talk (using notes if you want), lasting four to six minutes, on a subject on which there is more than one point of view. If you like, you can argue a line of thought, or you can discuss the various approaches.

2 Speak in a formal debate.

3 Read aloud or recite two contrasting passages of your choice, and use suitable voice techniques for each.

4 Chair a formal discussion or debate, and describe the duties of a chairperson.

5 Explain the following terms:

a   proposition

b   opposition

c. point of information

d point of order

e motion.

6 Listen to, or watch, a parliamentary debate, and discuss with the tester some of the techniques used by the speakers.

Date:...............................

....
Tester's signature Stage 1

....
Tester's signature Stage 2

....
Tester's signature Stage 3

....
Tester's signature Stage 4

....
My signature

SPORTSWOMAN

Before starting to work for this badge you must have been an active participant in your chosen sport for at least three months. When you start to work for the badge, you must decide which sport you are going to develop, and set targets for yourself over at least the next six weeks. Discuss these targets with your coach, teacher or instructor, and your tester before you begin. Complete one of the sections below.

Combat Sports (e.g. Fencing, Judo, Karate)

Proficiency points: six points for each award gained during the six-week period.

Attendance points: two points for each hour's practice (maximum two points a week).

1 Obtain a total of 18 points, either by attendance at a recognised club or class, or by attendance, plus awards gained since entering for the badge.

2 Show the equipment and clothing needed for the sport and demonstrate its use. Explain how to take care of it.

3 Tell the tester of your special responsibilities as a person having combative skills. Know the safety rules and why they exist. Demonstrate to your tester that you understand the rules, and the etiquette of your chosen sport.

4 *Either*

Gain a proficiency award.

or

Show the tester that you

are able to demonstrate techniques suitable to your grade in the sport.

5 Talk to the tester about the development of your chosen sport.

The tester should be a qualified instructor or coach.

Individual Sports (e.g. Archery, Golf, Trampoline, Gymnastics)

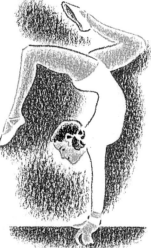

Proficiency points: six points for each award gained during the six-week period.

Participation points: two points for each practical session attended, either a match or practice (maximum two points a week).

1 Obtain a total of 18 points, either by practical participation, or practical participation plus awards gained since entering for the badge.

2 Show the tester the equipment required for your sport, and explain carefully the safety requirements when using it. Explain how you take care of and store your own and your club's equipment.

3 *Either*

Gain a proficiency award.

or

Perform a stated sequence of movements with good control and style.

or

Demonstrate techniques for scoring points.

The tester should be a qualified instructor or experienced club member.

Team Games (e.g. Netball, Rounders, Volleyball)

Proficiency points: two points for each representative match played (maximum two points a week).

Attendance points: two points for each squad practice attended (maximum two points a week).

1 Obtain a total of 18 points, either by attending squad practices, or by attending practices and taking part in matches during the six-week period.

2 Show the tester the equipment used in your chosen game, and explain how to clean and care for it. Wear your team uniform, and explain how you keep it all clean and tidy.

3 Demonstrate to the tester a variety of skills that you would use in the game such as dodging, tackling, marking, throwing, catching, hitting. You should show good control skills and neat footwork. Tell the tester of some of the skills that are important in the position that you play.

4 Tell the tester how points or goals are scored in your game, and the rules.

Racquet Games (e.g. Tennis, Badminton, Squash)

Proficiency points: six points for each proficiency award gained during the six-week period. Two points for each representative match played.

Attendance points: one point for each half-hour practice or coaching session (maximum two points a week).

1 Obtain a total of 18 points by attending practices, attending coaching, playing in matches or gaining proficiency awards.

2 Show the tester the racquet that you normally use. Tell the tester how you would choose a new one, and how you would look after the one you use. Wear your sports clothes and explain to the tester why you have chosen them.

3 *Either*

Gain an appropriate award.

or

Demonstrate to the tester how you would serve, play forehand and backhand shots, and play an overhand shot.

4 Keep the score accurately for a complete game. Explain to the tester the boundaries of the court and be able to tell when a service is good.

Date:.............................

....
Tester's signature

....
My signature

STAR GAZER

1 Keep a notebook or logbook over a period of three months giving observations of stars, moon and planets (if any) visible from a window, garden or street in or near your own home.

There should be at least one entry a week made regularly at about the same time in the evening.

Polaris
Pointers
THE PLOUGH

2 Demonstrate with diagrams, drawings or preferably models, the relative position and size of the sun, the moon, the earth and other planets; show their movements.

3 Point out in the sky at least:

a four constellations which are visible all the year round

b four constellations not visible all the year round

c four first magnitude stars; know to which constellations they belong and at what time of the year they are visible.

4 Find a compass direction from the stars.

Date:.............................

....
Tester's signature

....
My signature

STITCHERY

1 Make an article, such as an apron or scatter cushion, using fabric and decorative stitches in a creative way.

2 Make a picture using a variety of materials, threads and stitches or a toy or doll decorated with stitchery.

3 Bring to the test a sampler with at least eight different stitches, and be prepared to demonstrate any of these at the test.

Date:.............................

....
Tester's signature

....
My signature

SURVIVAL

Note *At all stages, the test should (as much as possible) be based on practical tasks, rather than theory. Suitable clothing should always be worn.*

Hint For further information, refer to *Improve Your Survival Skills* by Lucy Smith, published by Usborne and *Survival : A Complete Guide to Staying Alive* by Martin Forrester, published by Sphere.

Stage 1

1 Make an emergency shelter (you may ask someone to help you but you should give the instructions).

2 Demonstrate or describe a way of collecting water, e.g. a solar still.

3 Recognise three edible and three inedible plants (you may do this from pictures if you wish).

4 Show how to find north with a compass.

5 Follow a trail of 0.8 to 1.6km (0.5 to 1 mile), depending on locality. The trail may be of woodcraft signs, human or animal tracks, secret clues, etc. The tester may go with you.

6 Demonstrate or describe two methods of survival swimming.

7 Describe what you should do if you are snowbound in a car.

Stage 2

1 Demonstrate or explain the factors that should be considered when choosing and designing a site for an overnight shelter.

2 Know when and why water might need to be purified and demonstrate or explain two ways of doing this.

3 Gather wood, light a fire and cook a two-course meal.

4 Show how to find north without a compass.

5 Remain in the open for half an hour, moving as little as possible, and observe the animal, bird, insect and plant life going on around you. Describe this to the tester, saying what, if anything, would be useful for survival.

6 Know which garments to discard and which to retain when immersed in cold water in an emergency.

7 Know how to prevent, recognise and treat hypothermia. Describe the early signs of extreme weather conditions.

Stage 3

1 *Either*

Build a shelter that would stand up to wet and windy conditions for at least two nights.

or

Build (or explain how to build) a snowhole.

2 Describe four different ways in which you might find water for survival.

3 Demonstrate or describe two different ways of lighting a fire without matches. Explain which woods are good and which are unsuitable for lighting a fire. Light a fire and cook a two-course meal without utensils.

4 Demonstrate how you would take a compass bearing and convert it to a map for two of the following purposes:

a to identify a peak or some other geographical feature

b to work out your position through a resection

c to take the aspect of a slope to work out your position.

5 Describe at least three methods of attracting the attention of rescuers.

6 Know what to do in a car that has sunk under water.

7 Explain the importance of the following in cold weather conditions:

a food

b drink

c alcohol

d hygiene

e breathing though the nose.

Stage 4

1 Prepare an emergency survival kit. Explain to the tester why you have chosen each item, and how it could be used.

2 Know how to use and maintain an axe and saw.

3 Describe what you would do if you were lost in:

a a forest

b a mist in open country.

4 Do one of the following:

a Train one or more girls in the skills and knowledge necessary to pass a lower level of this badge.

b Set up an incident hike or survival trail for a group less experienced than yourself to follow.

c Negotiate with the tester a personal challenge that will test your resourcefulness and preparedness. (This could be undertaken with a group.)

Date:................................

....
Tester's signature Stage 1

....
Tester's signature Stage 2

....
Tester's signature Stage 3

....
Tester's signature Stage 4

....
My signature

SWIMMER

Note *The abbreviation STA has been used for the Swimming Teachers' Association and ASA for the Amateur Swimming Association.*

Stage 1

Note *The tester should be a qualified swimming teacher, your regular swimming teacher or a suitably experienced adult.*

1 *Either*

a Safely jump in from the edge of a pool.

b Bending your knees, submerge yourself in shallow water ten times, breathing out each time.

c Briefly sit on the bottom of the pool. Sculling is permitted.

d Push off from the side of the pool, showing a back glide, and regain the standing position.

e Swim dog-paddle or front crawl for 10 metres.

f Swim on your back for 10 metres.

g Swim either front crawl, back crawl or breast stroke for 10 metres.

or

Hold the STA Pool Frog 2 Award.

2 Discuss with your Guider the hygiene and safety rules to be followed when using a swimming pool.

Stage 2

Note *The tester should be a qualified swimming teacher.*

1 *Either*

a Jump in to deep water and tread water for 20 seconds.

b Scull in a sitting tuck position for 20 seconds, stretch out to a back float and then regain a standing position.

c With your body in a vertical position and your feet together scull with your hands and keep your mouth clear of the water for five seconds.

d Float on your back with your feet together for two minutes, scull with your hands to stay afloat.

e With a float, swim front crawl legs only, for 15 metres.

f With your hands behind your head, swim back crawl legs only, for 15 metres.

g Using a float, swim breast stroke legs only, for 15 metres.

h Swim either breast stroke, front crawl or back crawl for 25 metres.

or

Hold the STA Pool Frog 3 Award.

2 Swim 50 metres confidently and without pause, any stroke.

3 Discuss with your Guider the reasons for hygiene and safety rules at your regular swimming place.

Stage 3

> Diving to depths greater than 1.5 metres may damage your hearing. Diving is undertaken at your own risk.

Notes

* *If you hold the ASA Bronze Challenge or Scottish Speedo Swimming Award equivalent you may omit Clause 2.*

* *For the first choice in Clause 2 the tester should be a qualified swimming teacher. For the second choice in Clause 2 the tester should be a responsible adult with the relevant knowledge and experience.*

1 Discuss with your tester or Guider the accidents that could occur if people disregard the safety rules at your regular swimming pool and at fun pools.

2 *Either*

a Jump into deep water.

b Swim 10 metres followed by a surface dive and an underwater swim of 5 metres.

c Tread water in a vertical position for three minutes.

d Scull head first, feet still and near the surface for 15 metres.

e Swim 400 metres using two strokes, with at least 100 metres using one of the strokes. Climb out of the deep end without using the steps.

or

a Swim regularly for three months. Make or get a swim-fit card from your local pool and keep a record of the distances you swim. Show this to the tester.

b Challenge yourself to a 600 metres swim, making a note of the time it takes you to complete this. Aim to swim 600 metres in less time than before. Keep a record of the dates and times taken and show this to the tester.

c At the test:

* Without pausing, swim 200 metres using one stroke and then swim a further 200 metres using a different stroke.

* Tread water for two minutes.

Stage 4

> Diving to depths greater than 1.5 metres can damage your hearing. Diving is undertaken at your own risk.

Notes

* *If you hold the ASA Gold Challenge Award or the Scottish Speedo Swimming Awards equivalent you may omit Clause 2.*

s

• *The tester should be a qualified swimming teacher, except for Clause 1 which should be assessed and signed for by the adult involved, for example a club organiser or Unit Guider.*

1 Choose one of the following:

a Under adult supervision, assist a non-swimmer to gain more experience in the swimming pool on at least three separate occasions within a two-month period.

b Help at a swimming club or disabled swimming sessions on a regular basis for at least two months.

c Give an interesting presentation of swimming to another Unit from any Section. Your presentation should include the following aspects: fun, health, sociability, safety and skills.

2 *Either*

a Safely dive or straddle entry into deep water (1.8 metres minimum depth) and swim 100 metres in two minutes, using two different strokes with 50 metres of each.

b Tread water for three minutes with one hand raised above your head. You may change hands if necessary.

c Scull head first on your back for 10 metres, tuck, rotate 360° and return, sculling feet first.

d Swim 10 metres, perform a forward somersault without touching the pool floor and continue swimming for a further 10 metres in the same direction.

e In 25 minutes, swim 800 metres (at least 200 metres for each stroke) using three of the following: front crawl, back crawl, breast stroke, butterfly, Old English backstroke or side stroke.

f Climb out without assistance.

or

a Swim regularly and discuss personal swimming goals with your Guider, teacher or coach and, together, set yourself three new targets to achieve over the next three months. Show the tester records of this.

b At the test show the following skills:

• Safely dive or straddle entry into deep water (1.8 metres minimum) and swim 600 metres using three different strokes.

• Tread water for four minutes.

• Retrieve an object from a depth of 1.5 metres.

• Climb out without using the steps.

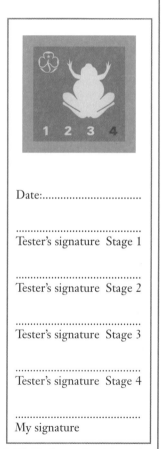

Date:................................

....
Tester's signature Stage 1

....
Tester's signature Stage 2

....
Tester's signature Stage 3

....
Tester's signature Stage 4

....
My signature

THRIFT

1 Tell the tester of at least three ways of saving money in the home on items such as food, household goods, cleaning materials, clothing and do-it-yourself projects.

Do one of the following:

a Make a new garment from an old one.

b Make a bed or cot cover from old or leftover wool or materials.

c Make any other useful article from second-hand materials.

2

a Describe in detail two methods of food preservation to be chosen by yourself from jam-making, fruit bottling, herb drying, food freezing and pickling. Take one example made by yourself to the test, being aware of its storage and future use.

b Bring to the test four recipes for using up

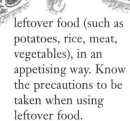

leftover food (such as potatoes, rice, meat, vegetables), in an appetising way. Know the precautions to be taken when using leftover food.

3

a Know ways of saving energy and natural resources, for example electricity, gas, oil, water, wood.

b Know the facilities for recycling waste in your area.

4 Be prepared to tell the tester about several small but inventive ways in which you yourself have been thrifty, such as using old cards, containers, materials etc.

5 Know the advantages of different ways of saving your money, for example, banks, building societies, the Post Office.

Date:...............................

....
Tester's signature

....
My signature

TOYMAKER

All your toys should be well made, safe and ready for use before you show them to the tester.

1 Make a toy of your own choice.

2 Do two of the following:

a Make a rag doll or animal of some soft material. Cut-out patterns may be used.

b Make a vehicle with movable wheels, from wood, cork or other material.

c Dress a doll, the clothes to be removable. The doll may be that submitted in Clause a.

d Make a room of a doll's house from a box; completely paint, paper and furnish it, using oddments and scraps.

e Make a scrap book for a toddler to handle.

f Make a model farmyard *or* doll's house *or* Noah's Ark.

g Make a mobile.

3 Make a study of the toys available in shops and give reasons why you think they are good or bad.

Date:............................

....
Tester's signature

....
My signature

ULSTER FOLK

Hint Information is available from The Guide Association, Province of Ulster, 38 Dublin Road, Belfast BT2 7HN.

1 Do one of the following:

a Read a book about St Patrick and then tell the tester what you have found out.

b Visit some of the places in Ulster associated with the life of St Patrick and share your discoveries with your Patrol.

c Visit a local folk museum and present your discoveries in an interesting way.

2 *Either*

Make a scrapbook or some visual display to illustrate interesting features of Ulster e.g. scenery, traditions and main occupations of residents.

or

Collect at least ten pictures or make drawings to illustrate life in your area through the ages.

3 Do one of the following:

a Play a folk tune on any instrument of your choice.

b Learn a folk song and sing it by yourself or with your Patrol or Unit.

c Perform a solo jig or set dance or teach your Patrol or Unit a simple team dance.

4 *Either*

Tell or act out, with your Patrol if necessary, a story about Cuchillain, Finn McCool, Oisin, Deidre, The Children of Lir or a similar subject.

or

Find the meaning of ten local place names and explain them to the tester.

5 Do two of the following:

a Cook a traditional dish, such as yallowman, soda bread, Irish stew or another dish agreed with the tester.

b Make a mat, collar or an edging strip in crochet lace, incorporating roses or shamrock motifs.

c Make a harvest knot, St Brigid's Cross or a traditional 'corn dolly'.

d Design a Celtic brooch and colour it in, or decorate the initial letter of your name with a Celtic pattern.

e Embroider an article using drawn thread work or patchwork.

f Make an article using a rag rug technique.

Date:..............................

....
Tester's signature

....
My signature

WALKING

Note *Adults will need to accompany you or supervise you on the walks as appropriate. The tester should be approved by the Division Commissioner.*

Hints

- **The definitions of the four categories of countryside for which the Walking Safely Training Scheme provides training can be found in** *The Guiding Manual* **and** *Qualifications,* **both published by The Guide Association.**

- **Details of your walks can be recorded in** *The Walking Safely Training Scheme Record Book,* **published by The Guide Association.**

Stage 1

1 Show the tester that you know how to dress to go on a walk. Be able to show your bag or rucsac and what you carry with you.

2 Go on four walks, one of which should be at least 5 km (3 miles) long. Make a brief record of each walk to include:

a the date

b the weather

c where you went.

You may use any method – such as photos, drawings, postcards, a tape or a play – in order to record the walk.

3 Know the eight points of the compass and show the tester where North is marked on simple maps.

4 Show that you understand the Green Cross Code and the Country Code. To do this you may devise a play or draw a chart etc. in your group.

5 Go for a short walk with the tester. You can plan this with the tester and anybody else being tested. Talk about interesting things you see on the way.

Stage 2

1 Be able to show the tester that you have thought about clothes and footwear for walks in different kinds of weather and area. Show what you would pack in your rucsac.

2 Make up a simple first aid kit. Know how to treat cuts, grazes, stings, blisters and sprains. Be aware of the effects of the sun.

3 Go on at least five walks, one of which should not be less than 10 km (6 miles) long.

Make a simple record of:

a   where you went

b   who was in the group

c   the date and weather

d   the distance covered

e   the purpose of the walk

f   the time taken

g   anything interesting.

4 Show a basic understanding of how a Silva compass works and be able to walk along simple bearings.

5 With the tester and others to be tested, plan a route using suitable maps. These might have a scale of 1:50,000 or 1:25,000, or be local sketch maps. Show your ability to follow a section of the maps. While you are on the walk, show an understanding of relevant Green Cross, Country and Water Safety Codes.

Stage 3

1 Show the tester your clothing and footwear, and be able to explain why you chose those particular items. Also show your waterproofs, personal first aid kit, emergency rations and emergency equipment. Tell the tester when and how you would use these.

2 Demonstrate your knowledge of first aid.

a   Know how to deal with choking.

b   Be able to deal with grazes, stings, sprains and the effects of heat.

c   Understand when not to move a casualty and when to call for extra help.

3 Participate in at least six walks, one of which should be no less than 15 km (9 miles) long and one,

if possible, should be to a height of 350 metres. Explain the purpose of each walk to the tester. Keep a record of the walks and include:

a   a description of the route

b   a route card to show distance and timing

c   the OS number of the map used

d   details of the group

e   emergency procedures, such as escape routes and telephone numbers.

4 Demonstrate your map skills.

a   Be able to give six-figure grid references from a 1:25,000 or 1:50,000 map, and show an understanding of the symbols used.

b   Set the map using a Silva compass and features. Be able to tell the tester the direction of different features in relation to others (grid bearings).

5 Using a 1:25,000 or 1:50,000 map, prepare a route card showing grid reference, height, distance, estimated timing and escape route. With a group, take the tester on this route (or meet her/him along it). The route should be at least 12 km (7 miles) long in Medium country or above (possibly valley bottoms in Difficult country).

Stage 4

1 Bring to the test correct clothing and equipment, including emergency gear, for Medium to Difficult country.

2 Demonstrate your knowledge of first aid.

a   Demonstrate artificial respiration.

b   Demonstrate pulmonary resuscitation.

c   Be able to put someone in the recovery position.

d   Recognise the signs

99

and symptoms of hypothermia and know how to deal with the situation.

e Explain how to deal with choking.

f Know when it is necessary to request emergency help and how much first aid you yourself should give.

3 Keep a record of the walks that you have completed. Your walks should include four full days in hill country ascending to at least 400 metres on each day. Your record should comprise:

a a sketch map, description or copy of the route

b an account of the purpose of the walk

c the route card

d notes on the walk, including date and weather conditions

e observations of land use, vegetation, geology, etc.

4 At the test, prepare a route card to include the following: grid reference, height, distance, magnetic bearings, alternative routes and timing. Use the card to demonstrate your ability to find your way in unknown country, using a map and compass.

5 Using either a 1:50,000 or a 1:25,000 map – or both – point out to the tester land forms commonly associated with upland areas and explain their significance to the hill walker. Repeat this exercise on the ground, as far as possible.

6 Know the Country Code and Water Safety Code and read *Safety on Mountains*, produced by the British Mountaineering Council and available from The Guide Association Trading Service. Explain to the tester the following:

a How the hill walker can contribute to the conservation of upland areas and understand the importance of public rights of way, permissive paths, access land and the reasons for restrictions.

b How to obtain information about an area, including local weather forecasts and information about rescue posts.

c The effect that physical features might have on weather conditions, group morale and speed of travel.

Date:...............................

....
Tester's signature Stage 1

....
Tester's signature Stage 2

....
Tester's signature Stage 3

....
Tester's signature Stage 4

....
My signature

WATER SAFETY

Note *The abbreviation RLSS UK has been used for the Royal Life Saving Society of the United Kingdom throughout this syllabus.*

Stage 1

Notes

• *If you hold the RLSS UK Rookie Lifeguard Two Star Core Award for Water Safety you may have this badge.*

• *The tester may be any responsible adult with relevant, up-to-date knowledge.*

1 Explain why water outside (e.g. lakes, rivers, canals and ponds) can be dangerous.

2 Explain why shallow water can be dangerous.

3 Explain why cold water can be dangerous.

4 Show an understanding of safety signs and flags.

5 Discuss locations where people could drown.

6 Explain where the safest places to swim are and why.

7 Explain why you must never swim alone.

8 Know the Water Safety Code.

9 Be aware of the different causes of water pollution.

Stage 2

Notes

• *If you hold the RLSS UK Rookie Lifeguard Three Star Core Award for Water Safety and do Clause 6, you may have this badge.*

• *The tester should be a person holding a current lifesaving award, a lifesaving teacher, a swimming teacher or a responsible adult with relevant up-to-date knowledge and experience.*

All parts of this badge may take place on dry land, including Clause 6. You may take this badge even if you cannot swim.

1 Know and understand the Water Safety Code.

2 Name two possible dangers involving water in or at each of the following:

a gardens
b parks and boating pools
c swimming pools
d farms and countryside
e rivers, canals and streams
f reservoirs and lakes
g beaches.

3 Discuss with the tester the problems of water pollution and water-borne diseases. What precautions can you take?

4 Explain why swimmers are more likely to drown than non-swimmers.

5 Choose one of the following:

a Give a five-minute presentation on water safety to your Unit.
b Produce a water-safety booklet for your Unit.
c Design and make a water-safety poster and display it at your meeting place, school or library.

6 Demonstrate the following rescues using methods approved by the RLSS UK:

a reaching with a rigid aid
b reaching with an article of clothing
c throwing a rope 5 metres to a person
d throwing a buoyancy aid 5 metres to a person.

Show and explain how to keep yourself safe while conducting these rescues.

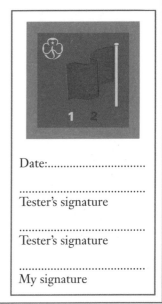

Date:..............................
....
Tester's signature
....
Tester's signature
....
My signature

101

W WEATHER

Hint You will find the following books useful: *The Weather* by Francis Wilson and Felicity Mansfield, published by Usborne and *Weather* by Tony Potter, published by the BBC.

1 Make a simple version of one of the following:

a   rain gauge

b   wind vane

c   wind sock

d   anemometer

e   barometer.

Use it in keeping your records for Clause 2.

2 Keep a record of the following for 30 days (consecutively if possible):

a   wind force (Beaufort Scale) or speed and direction

b   clouds (type and amount)

c   temperature

d   precipitation (rain or snow)

e   sunshine

f   any other conditions (e.g. fog, frost)

g   air pressure.

See if any patterns emerge (e.g. is rain more likely with a particular combination of wind direction and air pressure?)

3 *Either*

a   Know six weather sayings and test their accuracy from your own observations.

or

b   Know how to use your own observations of weather conditions to make a forecast.

4 *Either*

a   Explain the meanings of the following terms:

- warm front
- cold front
- occluded front
- cyclone
- anticyclone
- isobar.

or

b   Know the meanings of the symbols shown on a television or newspaper weather map.

5 Choose three of the following and explain, or demonstrate with simulations or diagrams, how they are formed:

a   clouds

b   dew

c   fog

d   hail

e   snow

f   rainbows.

6 Know where to get an up-to-date professional weather forecast for:

a   your own area

b   an area of wild country in a different area.

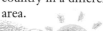

Date:................................

....
Tester's signature

....
My signature

WELSH FOLK

Hints
● Some useful reference books are listed below.

Songs of Wales Book 1 and 2 (edited by **Grancill Bantock, Paxton Music Ltd, Sevenoaks, Kent**)

Come and Dance (**Alison D Howie, University of Wales Press, Cardiff**)

Folk Dances – Llanover Reel (**The Gwynn Publishing Co, Llangollen**)

Welsh Whim and Other Dances (**The Gwynn Publishing Co, Llangollen**)

● **Information is available from Guides Cymru (The Guide Association of Wales) at Broneirion, Llandinam, Powys SY17 5DE.**

Note *Welsh or English may be used at the test unless the tester states otherwise.*

a Know the Welsh National Anthem (in Welsh).

b Know the composition of the Welsh flag and the story of St David.

2 Make a scrapbook to illustrate interesting features of Wales, the scenery, the main occupations of the people and the cultural traditions.

3 Do two of the following:

a Tell a Welsh folk story.

b Sing a Welsh folk song in Welsh.

c Take part in a Welsh folk dance.

4 Show a knowledge of the chief features and the purpose of the National Eisteddfod.

5 Dress a doll in Welsh costume.

Welsh costume patterns for 13cm (5-inch) and 25cm (10-inch) dolls are obtainable from the Welsh Training Centre, Broneirion.

or

Cook a national dish.

or

Make an article using a national craft.

Date:................................

....
Tester's signature

....
My signature

WINDSURFER

Note *The abbreviation RYA has been used for the Royal Yachting Association throughout this syllabus.*

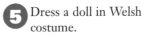

Notes
● *If you hold an RYA National Windsurfing Scheme Level 1 or an RYA Junior Windsurfing Scheme Level 1 and complete Clause 1 above, you may have this badge.*

● *The tester for Clauses 2 to 5 should be an experienced windsurfer over the age of 16. This person may also test Clause 1.*

1 Swim 50 metres and stay afloat for five minutes wearing clothes. This may be done in a swimming pool and you may wear a buoyancy aid if you wish.

2 Wear suitable clothing and buoyancy aid and explain to the tester why these are important.

3 Carry and launch the board and rig separately and raise the rig (with assistance if required).

4 Sail the board across wind, upwind and downwind. Do a 180° turn, basic tacking and gybing. Stop the board.

5 Dismantle the rig while afloat, roll it up and paddle back to shore.

Stage 2

Notes

• *If you hold an RYA Junior Windsurfing Scheme Level 2 or an RYA National Windsurfing Scheme Level 2 and do Clause 1 you may have this badge.*

• *The tester for Clauses 2 to 8 should be an experienced windsurfer approved by the County Assistant Outdoor Activities Adviser (Boating).*

1 Swim 50 metres and stay afloat for five minutes wearing clothes. This may be done in a swimming pool and you may wear a buoyancy aid if you wish.

2 Wear suitable clothing and a buoyancy aid and be able to discuss your choice with the tester.

3 Name the main parts of the board. Rig a

board demonstrating the use of knots and a safety leash.

4 Show that you can, with assistance if required, launch the board and rig connected at the water's edge, get onto the board in shallow water and sail away, return to shore in control, and remove the board from the water.

5 Sailing a set triangular course in winds of at least 8 knots, show an awareness of the three basic rules of the road and that you are competent in the following techniques:

a steering using body weight and rig

b altering the daggerboard

c sail adjustment, board balance and trim

d tacking

e gybing.

6 Know, and if possible demonstrate, how to be towed by another windsurfer and by a safety boat.

7 Describe five methods of self rescue and

demonstrate two. Know the distress signal.

8 Be able to explain the 'seven common senses' and how you would choose a safe sailing area, taking into account cover wind direction, water state, tides, Beaufort scale and personal limitations.

Stage 3

Notes

• *If you hold an RYA Junior Windsurfing Scheme Level 3 or an RYA National Windsurfing Scheme Level 3 and complete Clause 1 you may have this badge.*

• *The tester for Clauses 2 to 4 should be an RYA Windsurfing Instructor or hold a qualification approved by the County Assistant Outdoor Activities Adviser (Boating). This person may also test Clauses 1 and 5.*

1 Swim 50 metres and stay afloat for five minutes wearing clothes. This may be done in a swimming pool and you may wear a buoyancy aid if you wish.

2 Present yourself for the test wearing suitable clothing and buoyancy aid, and show that you can check whether equipment is safe and suitable. Explain how you would choose a safe sailing area and show a knowledge of local conditions and hazards.

3 Demonstrate that you are competent in the following techniques:

a **Rigging**
  • Rig various types of sail with assistance if required and know in which order to de-rig.
  • Know the types of harness line available.
  • Know how to position and adjust harness lines.
  • Know the correct adjustment of footstraps.

b **Launching, starting and landing**
  • Carry and launch a rig, assembled with

assistance if required.

- Beach start in stronger winds and control the board in shallows.

- Uphaul a rig and start in stronger winds.

- Come ashore under control and land in stronger winds.

- Know how to care for equipment ashore and afloat.

c Sailing techniques and stance
Demonstrate:

- Correct harness adjustment, hooking in and out in stronger winds.

- Efficient planing stance when hooked in.

- Basic footstrap technique (getting in and out of at least one).

- The beginnings of footsteering with daggerboard retracted.

- Awareness of the purpose of mast track and how to adjust it.

- 'Railing' upwind.

d Manoeuvres
- Tack in stronger winds.

- Gybe in stronger winds with daggerboard up.

e Freestyle
- Demonstrate three freestyle manoeuvres.

f Rescue
- Demonstrate being towed in stronger winds.

- Know, and if possible demonstrate, how to tow a board with rig and person.

4 Know how to deal with emergency situations – self help and getting help.

5 Know how to recognise and deal with hypothermia. Demonstrate how you would:

a stop bleeding

b identify and treat a broken bone

c treat an unconscious breathing patient.

Using a manikin, show how to give expired air resuscitation.

Date:...............................

....
Tester's signature Stage 1

....
Tester's signature Stage 2

....
Tester's signature Stage 3

....
My signature

WORLD CULTURES

Hint You will find lots of activities and information in *A World of Ideas*, published by The Guide Association.

To gain this badge you should complete five clauses. If you pass five more clauses you may have another World Cultures badge.

1 What would you include in a travel brochure that will attract people to visit your local area? Have a go at making one yourself.

2 Cook at least one course of your favourite meal. Make a list of the ingredients and find out where they came from. Locate all the countries on a map of the world.

3 Choose three well-known women of different nationalities in the fields of politics, acting, pop and rock, history or sports. Find out something about them and explain the reason for your choice.

4 Listen to, go to see or share in making music from another culture – e.g. a ceilidh band, calypso band, steel band, world music etc. What makes it special and appropriate to its country of origin?

5 Find out about a festival or celebration involving light or candles such as Hanukkah, Diwali, Loi Krathong or Advent. Make something, e.g. a diva, special candle, for that festival.

6 Have a fashion show with costumes from different parts of the world.

7 Face and body painting is very popular in many parts of the world. Try face painting or mehindi decoration on your hands or feet. Find out who would use it and when.

8 Play a traditional board game from another country.

9 Make a model or soft toy of an animal or a plant from another country.

10 Make a kite (traditional in China, Japan and Thailand) and fly it. Find out about kite festivals.

11 Puppetry is a very strong tradition worldwide. Find out about this e.g. shadow puppets from Indonesia. Make puppets and use them to tell a traditional story to Brownies or Rainbows or to the rest of your Unit.

12 Make a meal from another country. Try to use authentic cooking methods and eating utensils.

Date:...........................

....
Tester's signature

....
My signature

WORLD GUIDING

Note *To gain this badge you should complete five clauses. If you pass five more clauses you may have another World Guiding Badge.*

Hint You will find lots of activities and information in *A World of Ideas*, published by The Guide Association.

1 Guides all around the world sing 'Taps'. Learn Taps in another language and sing it at the end of your Unit meeting.

2 Find out about getting a Guide penfriend. Send a letter to a Guide abroad. This could be organised through the Post Box Secretary. See *The Guide Handbook* for details.

3 Girl Scouts in the United States of America sell cookies every year to raise money. Make some cookies or sweets, sell them and send the proceeds to The Guide Friendship Fund.

4 Make and play a game based on the World Badge and/or World Flag and know what each part of the Badge and Flag stands for.

5 In some countries Guiding has been suppressed for political reasons and Guides had to hide their uniforms etc. What six items would you choose to hide, to keep the Guiding spirit alive and why?

6 Imagine that you are at one of the World Centres. Design and write a postcard to your Patrol at home. You should include such things as the weather, people you have met, food and your journey.

7 Invite someone who has visited one of the World Centres or an international camp to come and talk to your Unit or Patrol about their visit.

8 Dress yourself or a friend in the uniform of a Guide from a WAGGGS Region other than Europe. You could adapt your own clothes or use paper etc.

9 *Either*

With your Patrol or Unit, celebrate Thinking Day in an unusual place.

or

Take part in 'Thinking Day on the Air' or 'Jamboree on the Air'.

10 Give or send a Friendship Badge to someone who lives abroad and tell them what it means.

11 *Either*

Take part in an international camp in the UK or abroad.

or

Host or entertain a Guide from another country.

12 Start a campfire blanket, or if you already have one, explain where the badges came from. Which badges can you swap or give to others if you go abroad?

Date:.............................

....

Tester's signature

....

My signature

WORLD ISSUES

Note *To gain this badge you should complete five clauses. If you pass five more clauses you may have another World Issues Badge.*

Hint **You will find lots of activities and information in** *A World of Ideas*, **published by The Guide Association.**

1 Many paper products are now made from recycled paper. Find and show three different products to the tester and

either

Make your own recycled paper.

or

Make a birthday card for one of your friends using recycled paper and materials.

2 Keep a diary of journeys you make during a week. What are the most environmentally friendly methods of transport?

3 Fill a container with as much water as you can safely manage and carry it for at least 20 metres. In many parts of the world women carry water every day. Discuss in your Patrol ways this task could be made easier.

4 In a group, play a co-operative game. How do co-operative games differ from competitive ones? Why is it important to co-operate? How can you apply this to situations between different countries?

5 Imagine that you are one of the first people to visit the inhabitants of a distant planet. As your ship is so small, you can only take ten things with you that would be typical of the

people on Earth. Collect the ten things that you would take and explain why you have chosen them.

6 Choose three different newspapers and cut out all the articles which mention other countries in them. Compare how much information is given in each paper. Are the different countries represented in different ways?

7 Find out about as many peace symbols as you can. Why were things like the olive branch and the dove chosen? Design and make a mobile using peace symbols.

8 Try out three different forms of non-verbal communication and send a message using one of them.

9 Find out about two simple ways that the health of people in developing countries can be improved, or lives saved.

10 Play a game about international justice or fairness, such as the Trading Game, the Paper Bag Game etc.

11 Identify several rights that you feel everyone in the world should be entitled to, e.g. the right to enough food. Choose three of these rights and make a poster using pictures, photos etc. to illustrate them.

12 Watch a TV programme, film or video about the work of an international organisation like WWF, UNICEF. If possible do something to help them.

Date:.............................

....
Tester's signature

....
My signature

WORLD TRAVELLER

Note *To gain this badge you should complete five clauses. If you pass five more clauses you may have another World Traveller Badge.*

> **Hint You will find lots of activities and information in *A World of Ideas*, published by The Guide Association.**

1 Find out what £1 sterling is worth in six different countries. Find out how you can change money into a foreign currency and how travellers cheques work.

2 Design a welcome poster in languages other than your own to make international visitors feel at home.

3 Make a list of medical facts about yourself, including any allergies or vaccinations. Why would this be a useful list to keep with a passport? Know where to find out about vaccinations you may need when travelling abroad and what basic medications to take with you.

4 Know when you need to have a passport and how to get one. What is a Guide Introduction Card, how do you obtain one and how do you use it?

5 Plan and make a journey to a place of interest or somewhere you would like to visit for a day. Plan a timetable, work out all the travel arrangements, eating arrangements, cost of entry fees etc. Think about safety and emergency contacts.

6 Cook an international dish on a lightweight stove, such as you would use if you were travelling, or make a packed lunch using foods from another country.

7 Make up two games you and your family or friends could play when travelling, one suitable for a car journey and one for a train journey.

8 Pack a suitcase with all the things you think you would need when travelling to a tropical country. What else would you need?

9 Plan and make a visual record of a journey, using e.g. postcards, photographic slides, prints or video. Compare these methods for cost, quality and possible uses.

10 Record in sound, or scents, the story of a journey.

11 Find an item representative of your local area that could be sent abroad as a gift. Package it and find out how it could be sent safely abroad.

12 Visit a chemist and see what range of sun-care products are available. Know what skin type you are. What are the dangers of not being protected?

Date:................................

....
Tester's signature

....
My signature

WORLDWIDE

To gain this badge you should complete two clauses from each of the World Guiding, World Traveller, World Cultures and World Issues badges.

or

If you have already gained the World Guiding, World Traveller, World Cultures and World Issues badges, you may have this badge.

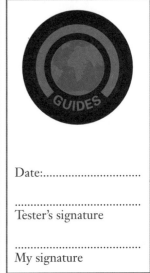

Date:................................

....
Tester's signature

....
My signature

W WRITER

Note *All written pieces should be sent to the tester in advance. They should be accompanied by a statement from the girl's parent, teacher or Guider confirming that they are her own unaided work.*

Stage 1

1 Write one of the following:

a a poem of not more than 20 lines

b a story of your own

c a song (choose a well-known tune) that could be sung by your Unit – for example, at a concert or on Holiday/Camp.

2 *Either*

You have just been carol singing, taken part in a sponsored walk, gone to London for the day or taken part in a similar event. Write a letter telling a friend all about it.

or

Keep a diary for a month. As well as noting facts note what you did and where you went, and try to include some of your thoughts and feelings.

3 *Either*

Make up a simple glossary (words and their meanings) of at least 25 words to do with one of your favourite activities (for example, Brownies or Guides, cooking, bird watching).

or

Write a letter inviting someone to your Unit's next Promise Ceremony explaining what the ceremony is all about.

Stage 2

1 Write two of the following:

a a fictional story of 800 to 1,000 words

b a portrait in words of someone close to you such as a parent, brother, sister or best friend (about 750 words)

c a true story (800 to 1,000 words) of something that happened to you when you were young

d an episode for your favourite TV 'soap'

e a collection of poems (at least five) around a theme, (for example, the seasons, colours or making friends)

f a dramatic sketch, lasting at least ten minutes, for the Unit to perform.

2 *Either*

Write a review (maximum 500 words), suitable for an

110

arts page in the press, of a play, film, exhibition, TV/radio programme or book.

or

Interview someone with an interesting job. Present the interview as a magazine article with a maximum of 600 words.

3 *Either*

Your Unit is putting on a pantomime to raise funds. Draft a letter to local firms asking for help with things like props, printing programmes, etc. Explain what your Unit is, what it does and what the money raised will be used for.

or

As part of a twinning scheme, some foreign Guides are coming to stay in your town or village. Write a letter of welcome (maximum 600 words), introducing the area where you live.

Stage 3

1 Write two of the following:

a a poem in a certain form, e.g. sonnet, limerick or haiku

b a radio commercial advertising a Unit event

c a short story (1,000 to 1,500 words)

d the synopsis of a play and its opening scene

e a descriptive account (1,000 to 1,500 words) of travels either in the United Kingdom or abroad

f a dramatised version of an event in history (performance time 15 to 20 minutes).

2 *Either*

Write a press release giving details about a forthcoming Unit event of interest to the public.

or

Write a 'letter to the editor' about a current issue.

3 Write a letter applying for an imaginary summer job, at home or abroad.

4 At the test be prepared to talk about your favourite authors and discuss whether they have influenced your writing style. Bring a review that you have written, of one of their books.

5 Bring to the test some standard reference books – e.g. a dictionary or thesaurus – and discuss how you use them.

Date:...............................

....
Tester's signature Stage 1

....
Tester's signature Stage 2

....
Tester's signature Stage 3

....
My signature

THE SERVICE FLASH

This Flash is awarded if you

Either

Carry out a regular service to or for others for a four-month period, e.g. a weekly service commitment to a club or group such as Riding for the Disabled, cleaning rota, crèche etc.

or

Are actively involved in a service project/projects to or for others for a minimum of 40 hours.

You may undertake a variety of service projects or be involved with one specific project. In all cases the service must be approved by your Guider and District Commissioner.

COLLECTIVE EMBLEMS

Arts and Crafts Emblem

Awarded if you gain five badges of your own choice from:

Artist
Band
Bellringer (any stage)
Carpenter
Confectioner
Country Dance
Craft
Dancer
English Folk
Entertainer
Flower Arranger
Knitter (any stage)
Knotter (any stage)
Manx Folk
Musician (any stage)
Music Lover
Needlecraft (any stage)

Photographer (any stage)
Scottish Folk
Singer
Speaker (any stage)
Stitchery
Toymaker
Ulster Folk
Welsh Folk
Writer (any stage)

If you hold two craft badges you may count them both towards the Arts and Crafts Emblem.

Date:...............................

....
Tester's signature

....
My signature

Fitness Emblem

Awarded if you gain the Fitness Badge and four badges of your own choice from:

Agility
Canoeist (any stage)
Country Dance
Cyclist (any stage)
Dancer
Dinghy Sailor (any stage)
Downhill Skier (any stage)
Oarswoman (any stage)
Outdoor Pursuits
Rider (any stage)
Sportswoman
Swimmer (any stage)
Walking (any stage)
Windsurfer (any stage)

If you hold more than one Sportswoman Badge you may count them all towards the Fitness Emblem.

Date:............................

....
Tester's signature

....
My signature

Little House Emblem

Awarded if you gain Child Care and Cook Badges (any stage), and four badges of your own choice from:

Care of Elderly People
Carpenter
Confectioner
Cooks (any stage)
Crime Prevention
Flower Arranger
Gardener
Handywoman
Homemaker
Hostess
Knitter (any stage)
Laundress
Needlecraft (any stage)
Thrift

Date:............................

....
Tester's signature

....
My signature

Science and Technology Emblem

Awarded if you gain Science Investigator and four badges of your own choice from more than one group:

Group 1

Aircraft
Bird Watcher (any stage)
Observer
Seasons
Star Gazer
Weather

Group 2

Carpenter
Computer (any stage)
Photographer (any stage)
Radio Communication

Group 3

Aquarist
Farmer
Forester
Gardener

If you hold two Farmer badges you may count them both towards the Science and Technology Emblem.

Date:................................

....
Tester's signature

....
My signature

Service Emblem

Awarded if you gain Emergency Helper, Accident Prevention and either First Aid, Home Nurse or Lifesaver and two badges of your own choice from:

Bellringer (any stage)
Care of Elderly People
Child Care
Conservation
Crime Prevention
Deaf Awareness (any stage)
Entertainer
Firefighter
First Aid
Home Nurse
Interpreter (any stage)
Lifesaver
Mapreader
Pathfinder
Road Safety
Sight Awareness (any stage)
Water Safety

Date:................................

....
Tester's signature

....
My signature

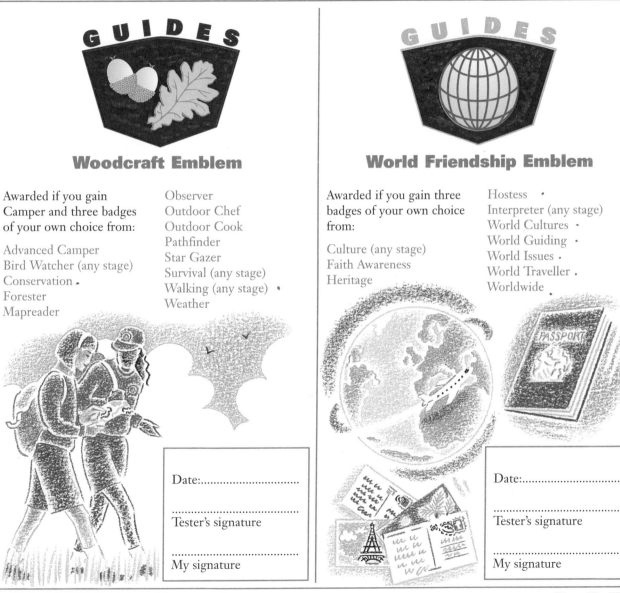

Woodcraft Emblem

Awarded if you gain
Camper and three badges
of your own choice from:

Advanced Camper
Bird Watcher (any stage)
Conservation •
Forester
Mapreader

Observer
Outdoor Chef
Outdoor Cook
Pathfinder
Star Gazer
Survival (any stage)
Walking (any stage) •
Weather

Date:..............................

....
Tester's signature

....
My signature

World Friendship Emblem

Awarded if you gain three
badges of your own choice
from:

Culture (any stage)
Faith Awareness
Heritage

Hostess •
Interpreter (any stage)
World Cultures •
World Guiding •
World Issues •
World Traveller •
Worldwide •

Date:..............................

....
Tester's signature

....
My signature

THE COMMONWEALTH AWARD

This Award is open to all senior Guides in Commonwealth countries. If you are 13 years of age or over you may start working on this syllabus as a Guide and complete it in the Guide or Senior Section.

The badge for this Award is metal and the design is the same throughout the Commonwealth. Once the Award is gained the badge may be worn on the sash for Guides and the badge tab for Ranger/Young Leader.

The County Commissioner is responsible for arranging the testing of the Award.

Syllabus

Clauses 1, 2 and 3 must be completed, together with two other clauses of the candidate's own choice.

1 History of Guiding

a Be able to talk about Guiding from its beginning at the Crystal Palace Rally in 1909, including the development of World Guiding.

b Know how Guiding developed in your own country.

c Know the basic aims and principles of Guiding.

2 Knowledge of the Commonwealth

a Know something of the development of the Commonwealth of Nations.

b Be able to talk knowledgeably about a Commonwealth country other than your own. Your knowledge should include:

- the day-to-day life of the people
- a little about the cultures and religions of the country
- how Guiding began and has developed.

c Do something practical in relation to the country of your choice, such as correspond with someone, or prepare a typical meal, or produce a scrapbook, or learn a craft, or make a collection of stamps, etc.

3 Service Within the Community

a Carry out service within the community. This should cover a total of not less than 40 hours over a minimum period of three months and within a maximum period of six months.

b Explain why you have chosen this particular form of service.

4 Health

a Know what health services are available in your own country. Find out what immunisation is required for entry into two other Commonwealth countries in an area of the world other than your own – this information should be correct at the time of taking the award.

b Explain how nutrition and sanitation can affect the health of your family.

5 Environment

a Study in detail one of the following within your own country:

- Conservation
- Environmental pollution
- Forestry
- Soil erosion
- Water supplies.

b Find out the environmental problems in another Commonwealth country and how that country is trying to solve them.

6 Cultural Heritage

a Know about the cultural heritage of your country under two of the following headings:

- art
- dance
- dress
- handicraft
- literature
- music – vocal or instrumental
- poetry.

Produce a collection of items such as pictures, programmes, instruments, books etc. for your chosen subject and discuss them with the assessor. Be able to demonstrate or perform in one of those chosen.

b Be able to talk to the assessor about three religions, denominations or faiths to be found in your country. You should be able to speak more fully about your religion, denomination or faith.

 Sport

a *Either*

Take part in or learn a sport new to you.

or

Demonstrate your knowledge of disaster preparedness.

b Have participated in a Guide camp of not less than three nights on each of two occasions within the past two years.

c Give the names of three outstanding Commonwealth performers in three different sports.

8 Public Speaking or Debating

Either

Give a talk to a Company or Unit on any subject you choose for not less than five minutes.

or

Take part in an organised debate being the principal speaker for or against the motion.

9 Creative Writing

Write a poem or story about life in your own country or tell a legend from your cultural heritage.

After acquiring the badge, the story or poem should be sent to your Association's Headquarters.

 Civics

Describe your system of government, and that of a different country in the Commonwealth.

11 Observation

The candidate should choose and complete any two of the following clauses:

a Observe some aspect of nature such as birds, animals, plants etc. over period of three months. Make a nature notebook and take it to the assessment ready to talk about your observations.

b Observe and make notes on at least two historical monuments/buildings and be able to tell the assessor interesting points you have noted.

c Talk to the assessor about the architectural developments in your country over a specific period, telling what you have observed for yourself and giving examples of the buildings.

d Tell the assessor of a drama, ballet or dance you have seen and be able to describe it.

Date:.............................

....
Tester's signature

....
My signature

GUIDE CAMP PERMIT

If you hold this permit you may take your Patrol to camp. If you want to take this permit it is suggested that you encourage and train your Patrol to take the Camp Preparation Patrol Interest Pennant.

Before taking this permit you must:

- be 13 or 14 years old and in a Guide Patrol
- be recommended by your Patrol Leaders' Council and District Commissioner
- hold the Camper Advanced Badge.

The Permit Test

This takes the form of a Patrol camp for at least two nights which you must organise and run. This includes planning and using the time so that everyone can enjoy all you do. The test may be taken during your Unit camp on the same or an adjacent site, providing you fulfil all the requirements as if your Patrol were camping on its own.

During the camp you must keep bedding and clothing aired and dry, store food sensibly, and see that meals are well cooked and served. Show the tester your first aid kit. You will be asked to show how to treat one of these: cuts, grazes, serious bleeding, burns and scalds.

You must be able to take good care of the tents and other equipment, and the site, and clear up well.

Conditions for Patrol Camps

If your Patrol is camping on its own (if not near your Unit camp) the site must be approved by the District Commissioner and Camp Adviser.

The camp must be in private grounds within walking distance of an inhabited house where there is an adult who undertakes to help if needed.

You may take three, four or five Guides with you, preferably members of your own Patrol, and one of them must have camped before. All Guides must be members of your Company. You may take up to seven Guides with you if all are members of your Patrol and at least two have camped before.

Each Guide must bring a permission form signed by her parent or guardian.

The camp must be for not less than two nights or more than three nights.

Swimming and boating is not permitted unless a qualified adult approved by your District Commissioner is in charge.

Date:...............................

....
Tester's signature

....
My signature

PATROL PURPOSE PATCH

Notes

- *While working for the Patrol Purpose Patch you should try to keep the same Guides in your Patrol. Your Patrol may work for and wear more than one Patrol Purpose Patch.*

- *This is tested by a panel made up of your Patrol Leaders' Council, including your Unit Guiders, and one other interested adult.*

1 As a Patrol choose four activities from your handbook which you could carry out as a Patrol. They should be from different chapters so that they cover four of the Eight Points of the Guide Programme.

2 Make plans for completing these items.

3 Report to your testers the items you have chosen and the plans you have made.

4 Carry out these plans within three months of reporting them. Each member of the Patrol must take a special part in at least one item.

5 When you have completed your chosen items report back to your testers. Each member of the Patrol must be prepared to talk about her contribution.

PATROL INTEREST PENNANTS

If a girl is genuinely absent the test can go ahead providing she can demonstrate her contribution in that area at another time. Where more than a quarter of the Patrol are absent the test will have to be re-scheduled.

CAMP PREPARATION

1 Pitch, strike and air a tent.

2 Make a fireplace out of doors, light a fire and cook on it.

3 Each member of the Patrol must roll and tie up camp bedding.

4 Make gadgets for sleeping tent, kitchen tent, wash tent. Improvise a flagpole.

5 Have a first aid kit and show how to deal with burns, scalds, cuts and sprains.

6 Plan, and at your test carry out an activity which can only be done out of doors such as making a shelter, playing a wide game, getting a Patrol across a stream without getting wet, making and using an outdoor oven, making something out of natural material.

Date:.............................

....
Tester's signature

....
My signature

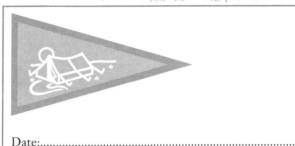

Date:...

Tester's signature...

My signature...

COMMUNICATION

Note *Separate clauses may be taken at different times, but you must complete the pennant within six months of starting.*

A Personal Communication

1 Use short sketches to illustrate the following aspects of communication.

a Positive and negative forms of communicating, e.g. what helps/prevents communication between people?

b The importance of communicating, e.g. situations where it is important to get the correct message conveyed, accurate facts etc.

c Verbal and non-verbal communication, e.g. body language, gestures, tone of voice, accent etc.

2 Alternative forms of communication.

Make up a sentence about your Patrol and communicate it to the tester in eight different ways, e.g. a foreign language, Morse, cartoons, signing, mime, Braille.

B Media Communication

1 Study the way in which news is presented on either the television, radio or in newspapers. Use this information to make up a news bulletin about your Patrol and its activities over a week. You can present this in one of the following styles:

- TV broadcast
- radio broadcast
- newspaper article.

2 Make up a game using adverts (pictures or words and music) and play it with another Patrol.

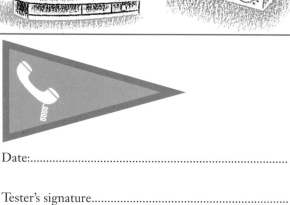

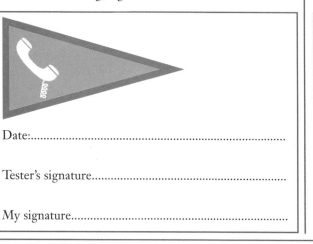

Date:..

Tester's signature...

My signature..

Date:..

Tester's signature...

My signature..

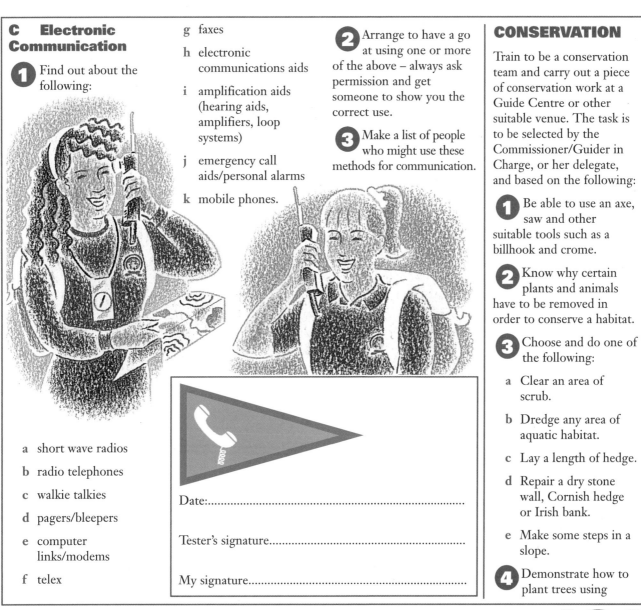

C Electronic Communication

1 Find out about the following:

a short wave radios

b radio telephones

c walkie talkies

d pagers/bleepers

e computer links/modems

f telex

g faxes

h electronic communications aids

i amplification aids (hearing aids, amplifiers, loop systems)

j emergency call aids/personal alarms

k mobile phones.

2 Arrange to have a go at using one or more of the above – always ask permission and get someone to show you the correct use.

3 Make a list of people who might use these methods for communication.

Date:..

Tester's signature...

My signature..

CONSERVATION

Train to be a conservation team and carry out a piece of conservation work at a Guide Centre or other suitable venue. The task is to be selected by the Commissioner/Guider in Charge, or her delegate, and based on the following:

1 Be able to use an axe, saw and other suitable tools such as a billhook and crome.

2 Know why certain plants and animals have to be removed in order to conserve a habitat.

3 Choose and do one of the following:

a Clear an area of scrub.

b Dredge any area of aquatic habitat.

c Lay a length of hedge.

d Repair a dry stone wall, Cornish hedge or Irish bank.

e Make some steps in a slope.

4 Demonstrate how to plant trees using

either the pit or T-notch method.

5 Show, while taking part in a conservation task, that you are aware of all the hazards involved in this type of task and that you have taken all necessary safety precautions to ensure your conservation team is a safe one.

6 Make a Patrol presentation to show the meaning of conservation to your Company, the general public or other interested groups.

Date:...

Tester's signature...

My signature..

EMERGENCY TEAM

Train to be an Emergency Team. At the test be able to deal sensibly, quickly and calmly with two emergencies chosen by the tester, one of which will be based on Clauses 1 and 2.

1
a Using a manikin or mask, demonstrate artificial ventilation by the mouth-to-mouth or mouth-to-nose method. Show how to place the patient in the recovery position in case he or she should vomit.

b Know when and how to use artificial ventilation and external chest compression, e.g. drowning, electrical accidents or smoke-filled rooms.

2 Know the signs and symptoms you would look for in the case of a fractured spine. Understand the danger of moving or handling a patient when the extent of the injury is not known.

3 With any available wood light a fire out-of-doors, and in not more than half an hour make a hot drink for four people.

4 Be able to:
a Stop severe bleeding with a pad and bandage.

b Deal with burns and scalds, including

treatment to guard against shock.

c Put on an arm sling and bandage an injured ankle.

5 Be able to hold the interest of a small child for 20 minutes, using paper folding, string games, improvised puppets, etc. Each member of the Patrol is to be involved.

6 Using four different methods send a message a total distance of 2km.

7 Set a map and use it to follow a route of at least 2 miles (3.2km).

8 Throw an unweighted rope to reach a person 10 metres away.

Date:..

Tester's signature..

My signature..

ENTERTAINER

To gain this pennant you must do Part I or Part II.

Part I

Give a short camp-fire programme to include:

a a song with descant or second part, or a round

b an item using portable instruments, home-made or otherwise c an item other than singing (such as mime, game, dance and speaking)

d an item emphasising the enjoyment of rhythm or beat (such as Maori stick game, a well-prepared yell, an action song)

e an item from overseas

f taps and a vesper or closing song.

Part II

Plan and present a programme of entertainment to last 10 to 15 minutes. This can be in the form of a concert, play, act of worship, puppet show, display or something similar.

The entertainment must:

a be a single production

b be suitable for your chosen audience

c include at least five aspects of the arts – such as music, drama, speech, mime, design, craft and dance

d contain a large proportion of original material

e be well rehearsed and of the highest standard the Patrol can achieve following a period of hard work by every member.

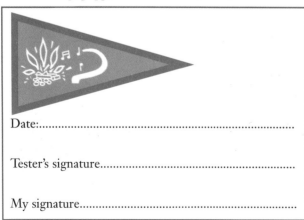

Date:...

Tester's signature..

My signature..

EXPLORER

> When you go on an expedition always leave details of your route with a responsible adult and always have a minimum of four people.

1 Get each member of your Patrol suitably clothed and suitably equipped for outdoor expeditions. Have ready a Patrol first aid kit and know how to use it. Have a working knowledge of the Highway Code (for pedestrians) and the Country Code. Get a Guider to check this when you are all ready.

Plan and carry out two expeditions. The first must be one of the options in Clause 2, and the second must be in connection with Clause 3. Afterwards give the tester an account of your expeditions.

2

a Climb a hill or high building and make sketches or take photographs of the views.

b Follow the course of an old trackway or river.

c Beat the bounds of the parish.

d Visit an historical building or other place or building of interest.

3 Track down the things listed below and bring some evidence of them:

a three plaques on house exteriors

b three old trade signs

c three interesting epitaphs or inscriptions on monuments

d three church brasses of historical interest

e two sites of archaeological interest

f four interesting buildings, each from a different architectural period

g four inn signs of interesting design or origin

h three buildings of local interest (such as old mills).

OUTDOOR COOKING

Note *The cooking should be mainly on wood fires, but you may use a stove as well if you wish.*

1 Cook out of doors and serve a two-course meal for the Patrol.

a The meal should include the following:

● potatoes, rice or pasta

● a vegetable

● fish, meat, eggs or another protein

● a cooked pudding

● a hot drink.

Convenience food may be used where sensible.

b While cooking the meal you should use some home-made cooking equipment such as an oven, haybox, barbecue, etc.

c Some of the cooking should be done without utensils.

2 Know the safety precautions for cooking out of doors on wood fires and camp stoves.

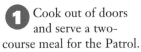

Date:..

Tester's signature...

My signature...

Date:...

Tester's signature...

My signature...

125

PIONEER

1 All members of the Patrol should:

a Know how to look after an axe and a saw.

b Learn the safety precautions for their use.

Show that at least one member of the Patrol can use an axe and two members can use a saw effectively and safely.

2 Make and use a rope ladder (this may have wooden rungs), or a simple rope bridge.

3 Make and use a swing ('haymaker') bridge or a transporter, or an A-frame ladder.

4 Choose one pioneering project which is not included in Clauses 2 and 3 to make and use. For example you could make a transport bridge, a stile, a raft or a ballista.

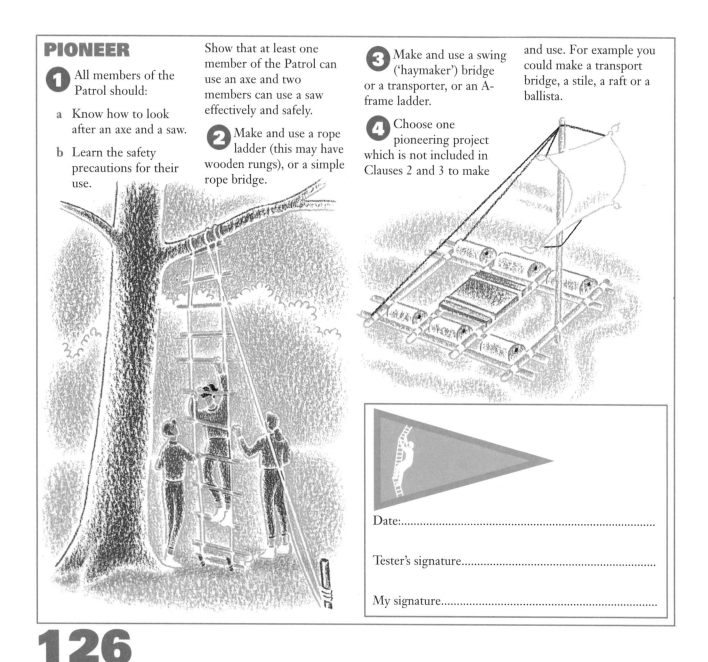

Date:..

Tester's signature...

My signature..

LIST OF BADGES

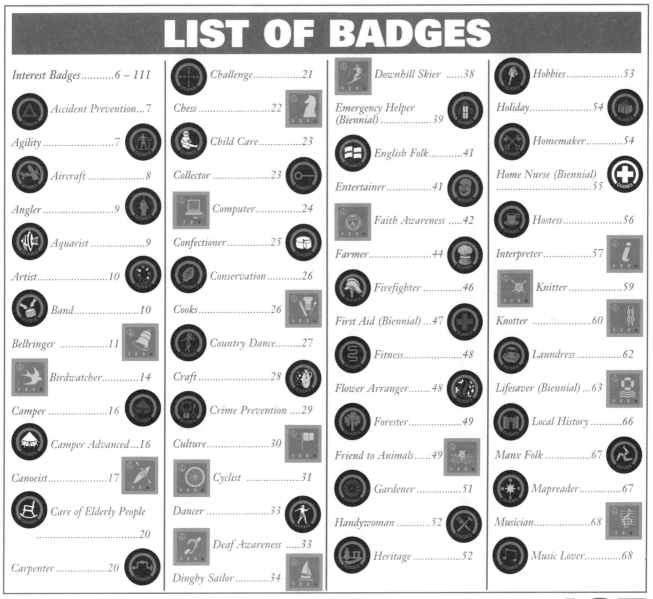